Orpheus Everts

The American System of Public Provision for the Insane, and

Despotism in Lunatic Asylums

Orpheus Everts

The American System of Public Provision for the Insane, and Despotism in Lunatic Asylums

ISBN/EAN: 9783743358157

Manufactured in Europe, USA, Canada, Australia, Japa

Cover: Foto ©ninafisch / pixelio.de

Manufactured and distributed by brebook publishing software
(www.brebook.com)

Orpheus Everts

The American System of Public Provision for the Insane, and

Despotism in Lunatic Asylums

The Ameri   ro-
vision fo
potism

By OI

[From the *America*   ]

THE AMERICAN SYSTEM OF PUBLIC PRO-VISION FOR THE INSANE, AND DES-POTISM IN LUNATIC ASYLUMS.*

BY ORPHEUS EVERTS, M. D(

A recognition of the fact that insanity is the result of physical disorder, which is not subject to the control or influence of will, and therefore constitutes a condition of irresponsibility, aroused a naturally strong interest in the minds of all thinking people in the welfare of the insane. This interest culminated, within the present century, in a general movement toward a public provision for the insane as wards of the State, including not only the care and custody of the person, but also the treatment of the disease. The various States of the American Union, following closely the plans adopted by older governments, began to make such provision, each for itself, near the middle of the century,† and since have carried forward the work with

---

* Read before the Association of Medical Superintendents of American Institutions for the Insane, at the annual meeting in Toronto, June, 1881.

† The Pennsylvania Hospital for the Insane was founded in 1750, and opened on February 11, 1752. The Provincial Assembly, after citing that " whereas there was frequently in many parts of this province poor, distempered persons, who languish long in pain and misery under various disorders of body and mind ; and being scattered abroad in different and very distant habitations can not have the benefit of regular advice, attendance, lodging, diet, and medicine but at a great expense, and therefore often suffer for want thereof, which inconveniency might be properly removed by collecting the patients into one common provincial hospital, properly disposed

increasing earnestness and activity. The provision which they have made thus far consists for the most part of one or more large hospital buildings in each State, built, officered and equipped, and wholly or in part maintained at the public expense. These buildings range in capacity all the way from three hundred to a thousand beds, with necessary room in addition for all needful officers and employés.

To these hospitals insane persons are or may be committed and admitted in conformity with specific statutes ordained for the government of the same and the protection of insane citizens. The general features of construction, organization, and management of these institutions are so similar as to constitute a "system," which consists of a "center building" for administrative purposes, and "wings" or extensions variously modified and subdivided into wards for the accommodation and classification of various grades of insane patients; and a board of trustees, or managers, appointed by the Governor, or Governor and Senate, or elected by the Legislature of the State, representing the authority of the State; a superintendent appointed by the board of managers, or by the Governor, representing the authority of the board; subordinate medical officers appointed by the board on nomination by the superintendent; and assistants of all grades, employed directly, or recommended for employment by the superintendent. The expenditure of public moneys

and appointed, where they may be comfortably subsisted and their health taken care of at a small charge, and by the blessing of God on the endeavours of skilful physicians and surgeons their diseases may be cured and removed," founded a "hospital for the reception and relief of lunatics and other distempered and sick poor, without partiality or preference."

In 1769, the Asylum for the Insane at Williamsburg, Virginia, was established, and in 1806, the Governors of the New York Hospital founded a branch, which was opened July 15, 1808, for the accommodation of the insane.

in the erection of these State institutions is limited in amount by legislative appropriation, being more or less ample, according to the liberality of views or general intelligence of legislative assemblies, the state of the public treasury, etc., and all expenditures for their support are under the managing officers and superintendents, who represent their respective requirements and necessities, and all under the direct sanction of law.

These institutions thus constructed and organized have for many years enjoyed a large share of public confidence, and have been looked upon by the people with a certain degree of pride and satisfaction. Public moneys were generally unhesitatingly appropriated for their construction and maintenance. Men of ability and general reputation for benevolence and integrity were selected and served as trustees or managers. To be selected and appointed medical superintendent was a professional distinction and a public honor. The recovery of a large number of insane persons at first committed to hospitals, and the improved condition of others made more comfortable by hospital treatment, magnified the reputation of hospital physicians, and exalted these institutions in popular estimation. State architecture, and State science for the benefit of the insane, did much toward redeeming their condition from its low estate, even among friends. The transfer of insane persons from local habitations, almshouses and prisons to places of such promise and repute, afforded relief and satisfaction to families and communities of untold value and acceptability. A fresh impetus was given to the study of psychology; psychiatry became an integer of medical science; cerebral physiology acquired enlarged importance. Disease of the brain and nerves assumed a leading position in the literature and practice of medicine.

With the multiplication of States and hospitals, these institutions became more and more familiar to the public eye. The number of recoveries and deaths never quite equaled the number of insane persons admitted to them. A gradual yet inevitable accumulation of the chronic and incurable class in hospital populations affected their reputation unfavorably as agencies of cure. A wonderful increase of population, natural and by immigration, produced applicants for public care and treatment more rapidly than the States could well make provision for them. Besides all this, accommodation was demanded for multitudes of variously incompetent persons, who had not previously been recognized as insane, or at least not so affected as to need hospital care. Insanity itself appeared, on a superficial glance, to increase in an undue ratio to population, and seemed to be less curable. Large and increasing appropriations to be disbursed by hospital officials did not escape the telescopic eyes of the *raptores*, the vultures and eagles of partisan politics. Aspirants for hospital positions, without especial regard to qualification or fitness of character, became more numerous and persistent, and as many of these institutions were drifted into the stream of politics, in some States, they even came to be looked upon as party spoils.

Coincident with these and other circumstances, a suspicion found lodgment in the public mind, and was cultivated by some, that the merits of these institutions never had been quite equal to their pretensions or their reputation. This suspicion, perhaps not altogether without ground, for hospitals were originally in some respects overestimated, multiplied and transformed itself, until it has become a formidable accusation, if not an organized condemnation of the whole system of public beneficence to which it pertains. To impute the worst characteristics of human nature to those most prominently employed in the administration of hospital affairs has become to a degree fashionable. To accuse managing boards of dishonesty, and medical superintendents and subordinates of incompetency, or criminal neglect of duty and abuse of authority toward helpless " prisoners," is a common feature of public scandal. Benevolent persons who, in their zeal, do not always distinguish between feeling and judgment, and are apt to accept earnest assertion for indisputable facts, have been moved to pity and indignation by the recital of such constantly repeated accusations. Men and women of intellectual and social distinction who may have themselves (unhappily) suffered the humiliation, and possibly some errors, of hospital treatment, after apparently recovering the use of their faculties, have given tone and color of veracity to stories of ill-usage, and vigorous expression to mental concepts of hospital administration, tinged by memories and imaginations, the morbid parentage of which may be unsuspected by others or even by themselves. Born agitators and " professional reformers," who live and move upon the borderland of insanity, being native there, or revolve on their own axes—who are ever intent upon turning the world upside down, and having things done some other way, no matter what the present way may be— have appropriated all such suspicion, imputation, accusation and scandal as valuable contributions to their magazine of munitions, to be used in a general crusade against whatever appears to be established. Professed neurologists and flippant neurospasts of the medical profession, arrogating to themselves all knowledge of psychology and psychiatry, have, by sneers, innuendo, and direct assault upon the character and qualification of medical officers serving in American hospitals for the insane, done what they could do toward the disparagement of hospital reputation. Hungry politicians of a low order, on the accession to power of a party which they had served, clamorous for "a change," have, in notable instances, unscrupulously manufactured and promulgated accusations and reports as testimony against incumbents of hospital places, calculated to disquiet and abuse the public mind respecting the management of these great charities. Foreign hospitals and their methods have been extolled and contrasted as in every respect superior to our own.

The American "system" of provision for the insane has been wordily arraigned, by some of these polemicists, who have obtained access to some of the most conservative papers and periodicals, and anathematised as an "unparalleled despotism." The American Association of Superintendents of Insane Hospitals has been denounced by the same class, and on the same kind of testimony, as "unscientific and selfish in character and purpose," "a close corporation" which has " tended to become a power as autocratic and domineering in asylum medicine and asylum politics throughout the Union, as are the authorities of each institution behind their own walls and locks."*

An association calling itself national has been gotten up ostensibly "for the protection of the insane and the prevention of insanity," but really for the purpose of concentrating and organizing hostility to present institutions and present methods, so far as they have been approved by a majority of those who have been or are at present engaged in administering them.†

---

* Dorman B. Eaton, *N. A. Review,* March, 1881.

† Dr. Hiram Corson, in a letter to the National Association for the Protection of the Insane, at a meeting held in Boston, says of the Association of Superintendents of American Institutions for the Insane : "Your counsel would be of infinite service in aiding our efforts to counteract the selfish,

This organization, which is not without talent and respectability, is seconded in its movements more or less by influential members of the medical and scientific press, and a miscellaneous support among the magazines and newspapers of the day. They have in some instances, under the guise of noticing the meetings of their self-constituted protection societies, crept into the editorial chair of the religious press, and there vented themselves of the most gross misrepresentations.

Such being the state of affairs at the present time, it may be well for all persons interested, officially or otherwise, in our public provision for the insane, to enquire into these matters, and ascertain, if possible, the origin and significance of these attacks. In order to do this systematically, it may be well to summarize what they all say on the subject. While those who criticise, complain and cry aloud against the American "system" of provision for the insane, do not all make the same allegations, do not all indulge the same spirit of hostility, do not all affect the same tone and temper of assertion, they do all agree in condemning present structures and present methods of administration; and assert they are unscientific and unsuccessful, always contrasting the institutions of America unfavorably with those abroad. It is said by them that American hospital buildings are too large,* too palatial, too

pernicious influence of this association. It may seem strange to you to hear me talk thus, but let me ask you what reform in the management of the insane has originated in that society? What but the invention and use of closer confinement, more means of restraint and seclusion of patients and determined resistance to the reforms urged by philanthropists who have witnessed how greatly they have ameliorated the miseries and contributed to the successful treatment of the insane?"—*Medical Record*, March 5, 1881.

* Dr. Crichton-Browne, one of the English Chancery Visitors, before the Parliamentary Committee, said: " I think pauper asylums may very properly be raised to 1,000, and that they will then work more efficiently and economically. * * * I have held offices in asylums of all sizes, containing from 100 up to 1,500 beds, and I think 1,000 the most economical number

expensively constructed; disagreeably monotonous in linear extension, and offensively prison-like in aspect. That American hospitals for the insane are appropriately adapted to but one class of patients, whereas there are several quite distinct classes of insane persons requiring a corresponding variation of general hospital provision. That American hospitals for the insane are practically inaccessible to the friends and natural protectors of their inmates, because of their great size, accommodating, each, the population of so large a territory. It has not been said directly, but one might legitimately infer from the tone and manner of complaint that has been made recently, that insanity itself has been increased in activity and malignity by the construction and occupation of American hospitals.

"Palatial asylums," says Eaton,* "constructed and furnished at an expense unparalleled in the world, and consigned to the almost absolute control of asylum doctors and trustees, have utterly failed to check the disease. * * * Year by year since their com-

---

if you have a sufficient staff. * * * I think in an asylum for 1,000 patients, one medical superintendent can keep up adequate supervision. Of course, of the 1,000 patients, there is a very considerable portion that are chronic cases that have been going on for some time, and that do not at all times need the special supervision of the medical superintendent. He has daily brought under his notice by the subalterns, any case that requires his special attention." To the question: "In those large asylums, the personal responsibility of the chief resident there is delegated to his assistant?" Dr. Brown replied: "No; the responsibility rests entirely with him.

Q. Relatively it must be smaller, and therefore he must depend more upon his assistants? A. Yes; but he has a large staff of assistants and subordinate officers. He is the head of the different departments, and everything that goes on is brought to his knowledge, I think, even better in a smaller asylum, where he is doing much departmental work, and perhaps a great deal of drudgery.

Q. The new registered hospital in Middlesex contains 2,000 patients, does it not? A. Two thousand, and Colney Hatch contains more than 2,000."

Speaking of the Lunacy Commissioners, he says: "The Commissioners would, I think, not place it below 600 now."

* Op. cit.

pletion, insanity has more frequently blighted our children, more broadly stricken middle life, more irresistibly tended to become chronic, more rapidly and certainly carried its victims to the grave." (??)

But all other criticisms and complaints pale before the culminant assertion of "unparalleled despotism" as the chief characteristic of administration, inherent in the American system of hospital government. A start-ling assertion when considered in its "naked deformity;" overwhelming when clothed in the garments of illus-tration. "Let us see," says the critic, "what this American system is, by showing the theory and method of governing the Asylum at Utica!" [One is tempted to pause and enquire, Why Utica? but the digression might prove more entertaining than the main line of investigation.] "Nine trustees, a majority of whom must reside within five miles of the asylum, are to gov-ern it. They make such by-laws and regulations as they deem expedient. They appoint the treasurer and the superintendent. They, by approval, determine the number of employés, and their salaries. They keep the only record of their own doings. They inspect their own work. They (or their subordinate, the superin-tendent) make all purchases. They audit their own bills. They report to the Legislature the only author-ized version of their own conduct. Neither their report, nor that of their subordinate, the treasurer, is required to contain such particulars as would disclose extravagance or any other abuses. As private owners of the institution, they could not have power more ab-solute and irresponsible." (Power enough, and just the power one would suppose, if entrusted to nine good and intelligent citizens, to insure a most excellent ad-ministration.) "But," our critic continues, "the author-ity of the asylum superintendent is, if possible, more dangerous and unchecked than that of the trustees. He is an autocrat—absolutely unique in this Republic; supreme and irresistible alike in the domain of medicine, in the domain of business, and in the domain of discipline and punishment." (We may rest for a moment here, long enough to enquire what has become of the nine trustees, with their despotic prerogatives and powers in the presence of this one man.) But to proceed. "He" (the superintendent) "is monarch of all he surveys from the great palace to the hen-coops, from pills to muffs and hand-cuffs, from music in the parlor to confinement in the prison-rooms, from the hour he receives his prisoner to the hour when his advice restores him to liberty." "This unparalleled despotism," continues our indignant protestant reformer, whose vision is by no means periscopic, who sees in the inmates of an insane hospital, at least the inmates of Utica, only languishing *prisoners* pitiably yet helplessly and hopelessly appealing to a heartless monster for liberty, "this unparalleled despotism extending to all conduct, to all hours, to all food, to all medicine, to all conditions of happiness, to all connections with the outer world, to all possibilities of regaining liberty, awaits those whose commitments may be easily unjust, if not fraudulent, * * * is over prisoners the most pitiable of human beings, whose protests and prayers for relief their keepers declare, and many good people believe, no man is bound to respect."

Behold the picture. Who does not recognize at once the great mogul of Utica, the head and front of hospital offending, closing the portals of his palatial prison house, as secure as Chillon, upon six hundred and odd of the most pitiable of human beings, "prisoners" and victims, shutting out all intrusion, trustees, commissioners, friends of the unfortunate, the great Empire State

itself, and there gloating over the anguish of the unhappy, and revelling in the enjoyment of his "unparalleled despotism?" What wonder that Utica has come
to be regarded by certain valiant knights as the castle
of an enchanter, whose dread power can only be dissi-
pated by tearing down its walls? The artist may deny
that this picture so accurately drawn, so boldly
modeled, so strongly lighted, so broadly treated, so
skillfully handled, so harmonious in tone, so deep and
yet transparent in color, so judiciously subordinated, so
perfect in action and so truthful in expression, was in-
tended for Dr. Gray! It is among the privileges of
art, if not the duty of an artist, to paint the possibilities of which a given combination of features is capable, and bring out hidden meanings which may lie be-
neath the superficial appearances of any subject. And
the picture thus presented may have been really in-
tended by the reforming artist to portray the features
and character of each and every superintendent of an
American hospital for the insane, however difficult it
might be for other than an artist whose ideal perceptions are not always, or necessarily, embarrassed with
material facts, to recognize the likeness. In all due
charitableness let us so accept it, and not for a moment
entertain the suspicion that any individual, or association of patriots and philanthropists, would commit the
folly of assailing the whole line of active force now engaged in administering the public charities of the
United States in the interest of the insane, for the sake
of covering an assault upon, to them, the gorgon-faced
"dread Hecate," who presides over the gloomy and
mysterious castle-keeps of Utica!

We need not indeed be harassed by such a thought,
inasmuch as the herald of opposition to the system, of
which Utica is but the illustration, has proclaimed the

responsibility of the American Association of Superintendents for all the defects and errors of the American system, and their perpetuation. "A system," pronounced as "vicious and defective for the care of lunatics—which excludes light and wisdom from without, and breeds and screens abuses within." A system, "compared with which the lunacy administration of European States is more economical, more humane, more effective for good." A system which, "ably and adroitly managed, has lulled and misled public opinion; shutting out light by arbitrary methods, defying exposure and change by the exercise of a despotic authority which ought never to have been conferred upon the managers of asylums." [Eaton.] Yes, that association, organized a generation since by thirteen as noble, conscientious, self-sacrificing and intelligent physicians as have ever ornamented the profession and humanity in this country; that association, without the embarrassment of a constitution or by-law, a rule of order, or a binding tenet, composed of men who have sought it voluntarily, for their own edification and profit, and the enjoyment of that perfect freedom of individual opinion and expression on every possible subject of interest which has ever characterized its discussions ; that association is now accused of having corrupted public sentiment, perverted public opinion, lulled public apprehension, hocus-pocused public legislation, "crystallized hospital despotism," and become itself a "crystallization of old methods and abuses," and "an obstacle to reform!" "It is not strictly a scientific nor even an orthodox medical society," says Eaton. "It has no analogies, so far as we know, in any other country," says the *Journal of Mental and Nervous Disease.* "It is a combination for mutual support and self-defense," says Eaton. "A trades' union rather than a scientific, professional association," echoes the *Journal of Mental and Nervous Disease.* * * "The members" of which "know, and feel compelled to keep, all the secrets of partisan favoritism, jobbing and extravagance, of which asylum trustees are guilty," says Eaton. Echo thus answers echo.

A formidable indictment, false or true! Is it true? True in part, but not wholly true? Is there enough truth in it to cast a shadow? Be it as it may, such accusations can not be "whistled down the wind." Persistent accusations, if undenied, become in time as effectual, in poisoning the public mind, as if sustained by proof. Let us consider these matters candidly. But, as a proper continent and basis of observation, let us affirm:

1st. Insanity, although it may be cosmopolitan in character, inasmuch as it is everywhere a manifestation of cerebral disorder, is not, Mr. Eaton to the contrary notwithstanding, cosmopolitan in the conditions of its successful treatment.

2d. Public provision for the insane and "lunacy administration" in the United States, do not differ more widely from the provision and administration of European States, nor contrast less favorably than do other and equally important institutions.

3d. All the peculiarities of the so-called American system, which by contrast appear as merits or defects, bear some definite and unavoidable relation to necessities or policies which are peculiarly American—and of a potential character, conspicuous enough, however readily overlooked by hasty or superficial observers.

Standing upon this platform, let us now freely admit that American hospital buildings are very large—much larger than the expressed opinion of the Association of Superintendents has justified. At the same time we

may as freely assert that in this matter, as in many
others of a public character, professional opinion has
often had to yield to the pressure of public policy,
determined by considerations of real or supposed necessities of state. The problem of public provision for
the insane by the American States, some of them habil-
itated with the sovereignty and responsibilities of States
but yesterday, has been, how to accomplish the greatest
good for the greatest number, not in accordance with
unlimited benevolence and unlimited means, guided by
unlimited knowledge; but with such means as might
be available for a given purpose at a given time, and
in accordance with ever present necessities and limitations. That large hospital structures, as compared
with much smaller, are conspicuously economical, can
not be denied. So that, when considered in relation to
territory, population, facilities for transportation and
other present and prospective circumstances, it can not
well be said that American hospitals for the insane are
injudiciously capacious. Until now even the older and
more wealthy States have not found it expedient to
provide State hospitals for all the insane of all classes
within their boundaries. Large hospitals furnishing,
as they do, a wider range for classifying inmates, are
more desirable as a limited provision, which must embrace inmates of all classes, than smaller structures can
be, both in a scientific and an economical sense. Large
buildings, when properly constructed with regard to
light, heat, ventilation and water-supply, do not suffer
in a sanatory sense, by comparison with smaller structures. Many of the American hospitals have been
doubled in capacity after years of occupation, without
adding to the ratio of mortality by such enlargement.
Take, for example, our favorite illustration, Utica.
Omitting the first year of its operation as insignificant,

the capacity of the asylum, as indicated by its average population for the next three years, 1844–5–6, was 265. The death-rate for that period, on the average population, (acute disease presumably preponderating) was 13 per centum. Ten years afterward, the capacity of the asylum, as indicated by population, was for three years, 1854–5–6, 405. The ratio of mortality on this increased population was 9 per centum. Within the next ten years the capacity of the asylum increased; the daily average population for the three years, 1864–5–6, being 598. The ratio of mortality for this period was 8 per centum. For the period 1874–5–6, thirty years after the first period mentioned, the capacity of the asylum was, indicated as before, 663, or more than twice as great as in 1844–5–6, with a *ratio* of mortality less than 9 per centum, against that of 13 per centum, when the population was not half so numerous. In estimating facts at their exact value, it is true that the death-rate of insane hospital reports needs to be considered in the light of many and varied circumstances. But, as these facts adduced are, or might be, corroborated by the history of nearly every large insane hospital in the United States, of ten or twenty years' standing, they may be accepted as conclusive testimony in their present relation.

If the assertion that large hospitals afford greater facilities for breeding and concealing abuses, has been verified by any instance, it could have been true only because of the expenditure of less money, and the employment of a smaller force of service in proportion to the number of patients accommodated than smaller hospitals require, and instead of being a probable fact, should have been a practical impossibility. Such a fault pertaining, as it must, to a special administration, should not be attributed to a system, and the testimony of results should be accepted as the best evidence of good or bad general conditions and management. For it is true that any general defect of conditions and appliances, including buildings—any diminution of administrative force below a requisite amount—any general neglect of well-ascertained duties of professional or personal attention to the insane, including matters of discipline, exercise, cleanliness, food, rest, amusement, medication and nameless minor matters of address contributing to common comfort; to say nothing of indifference to, and toleration of, unauthorized and inconsiderate seclusion or restraint of patients for the sake of convenience or punishment; or even "heroic medication" will soon manifest themselves in the tell-tale record, if honestly kept, of hospital mortality.

The cost of hospital buildings in America, whether extravagant or not, can only be decided by first ascertaining what the standard of value should be. If we are to consider American hospital building in the light of a barren necessity required for the purpose only of securing and sheltering the insane as so many unreasoning animals, then indeed they must appear to have cost enormously too much. If, however, we may consider them in the light of public beneficence, colored by the enlightened sentiment of an advanced civilization, founded and maintained for the purpose of restoring the lost integrity of human reason; succoring and sustaining the helpless, and protecting society from the dangerous, yet irresponsible, and especially if we may estimate at its true value the æsthetic influence which, by their stately architecture, they have exerted over the public mind, an influence which has reached and affected the insane mind through impressions made while in a state of health, we can not conscientiously and intelligently say their cost, as a system, has been too great. The cost of particular buildings, owing to particular circumstances, should in no wise touch the general statement.

The prison-like appearance of American hospitals for the insane is a feature which is more complained of by others than by those who are presumed to suffer from it. To be "behind the bars," sentimentally considered by sane persons, is a condition from which they shrink with abhorrence. But, as a matter of fact, the window-guard, if not clumsily or obtrusively constructed, attracts but little attention from the insane. Those who complain of "bars," in an insane hospital, generally are better off because of them; those who have no need of "bars" are indifferent respecting them.

A great source of error seriously affecting hospital reputation lies hidden in the fact that the changed condition, circumstances, needs, sensibilities and propensities of the insane are forgotten by the outside world whenever hospital doors are closed upon them. Even the most intimate friends of insane persons, worthy and intelligent people, as intelligence is rated, who may have exhausted the strength of their own patience and affection, vainly endeavoring to calm and control a maniacal or suicidal member of the family, as soon as they have delivered such member, bruised, perhaps, and scarred by ropes or irons or violent handling, to the more merciful restraints of an insane hospital, they begin to think of him or her as sensitively pining "behind the bars." Or, if wrought upon by some "reformer's" account of hospital cruelties, or a more dignified reviewer's essay on "despotism in lunatic asylums," they may fancy him or her painfully languishing in the horrible environments of a "Utica crib." Alas, unhappy Utica! Parent of all that is disreputable and offensive in hospital history, when will thy windows be opened to the light of wisdom from without? When will thy doors cease to slam in the face of pitying humanity and humble science!

But this coarse criticism of hospital architecture is but an overcoat to the more interior garments of asylum despotism called "physical restraints," which pertain more especially to the *personnel* of administration than to hospital architecture. By this token, the use or disuse of physical restraints, all hospital administration, as well as architecture, is to be recognized as evil or good, as successful or unsuccessful, and by no other. " *The degree of freedom from physical restraints,*" says the great North American Reviewer, " *is at once the test and measure of good asylum management.*" Abolish all semblances of physical restraint, remove all bars from windows, and all locks from doors of insane hospitals—destroy all camisoles, muffs, mitts, straps, strong rooms, and especially all cribs (which smell of Utica); domicile your madmen and imbeciles in cosy cottages, with pleasant outlook and garden privileges—establish for them schools, gymnasiums and work-shops—employ only educated saints in sufficient numbers for companions, teachers and comforters—withdraw all authority from the medical superintendent to prescribe or enforce rules or treatment, not previously suggested and approved by officers of "higher grades," unaccustomed to the care and treatment of the insane—appoint a series of officials, to watch over and report eachother's doings—remove such appointments from the reach of political influences—in short, reconstruct American society, abolish human nature, modify the conditions of cerebral disorder, and especially change everything relative to hereditary traits of character, education and habits of thinking, and ring in a millennium of lunacy, or be denounced as despots and obstructionists; is about the alternative presented to the managers of American hospitals for the insane at the present time, by men who demand that the public regard them as wise, and all who disagree with them as worse than foolish.

A further discussion of the use and abuse of restraint in the management of the insane would seem to be superfluous, yet it is persistently forced upon us. Certain it is, that whatever abuse of restraints is still to be found in hospital practice, in American institutions, it is not general, nor is it approved by medical superintendents, individually or collectively. If we are to believe the reports which they make of their own conduct, the use of mechanical restraints, exclusive of hospital buildings, is reduced to a low figure in American hospitals, and limited to exceptional cases, where, as a matter of professional judgment, such restraint is preferable to manual force of attendants, chemical restraints, or an unrestrained condition; a matter which does not involve the question of humanity, any more than does a matter of choosing between the use of zinc and iron, quassia and quinine as tonic medicines.

So too, respecting open doors, and the use of cottages as appendices to general hospitals, furnishing a cheaper or a more appropriate provision for mild, inoffensive, and variously imbecile patients; a class that has been gradually accumulating, and will continue to accumulate, with the growth of States, and without regard to the existence of sanatory institutions. There is no reason why such provision should not be adopted, and certainly no obstruction of a general or formidable character is being placed in the way of so innocent an experiment by "asylum doctors" or others.

But after all we have the question left—the great question—"human nature being as it is," of personal authority in the management of the insane. This "autocracy—anomalous and unique in this republic." *What of it?* The problem of authority, delegated or assumed, by which one man may control the actions of another, although the one may be wise and self-possessed and the other a madman or a fool, is never without interest to any man born of Anglo-Norman or consanguineous ancestors. As American citizens we are jealous of our unalienable rights, especially the right of self-control, and do not readily surrender them without contest, even though insane. It is true, also, that but few men are so generously endowed by nature, and so well self-poised by training, as to be safely trusted with the autocratic power which, within a certain sphere, is essential to the successful management of an insane hospital in America. It is for this reason that the most learned neuro-psychologist, the vainest neuropath, the most conspicuous instructor of the feeble-minded, or the most conscientiously |misinformed philanthropist, is not, *necessarily*, qualified to superintend an insane hospital, or to criticise judiciously the merits or the conduct of those who are so qualified. There is no other human relation, official or other, like that of a medical superintendent of an insane hospital .to its population. The conditions of his authority can not all be specified, because the conditions which he has to meet with authority can not be anticipated. His government can not be otherwise than largely personal, because the conditions requiring government are individual and personal. Large discretionary powers must of necessity be delegated to him. Yet, not larger or more dangerous than is delegated by common law and the statutes to the fathers of families, or the guardians

of wards, in all civilized countries, and for the same
general reason, viz., the irresponsible condition of those
who are consigned to him for government. It is true
that mistakes may be made in the selection of men for
superintendents. It is probable that the very best are
not always chosen. But a good administration can not
be secured through incompetent or even bad officials by
depriving them of authority to do that which must in
some way be done—nor need a bad administration be
expected of competent and exemplary officers because
invested with discretionary powers. To deny that such
powers may be and are. sometimes abused through
ignorance, or lack of the highest order of character and
qualification, would be to write oneself down "an ass."
That errors of administration, errors of professional
opinion and practice, undetected neglects of duty, de-
ceptions and concealments, and even exceptional cruelty
of conduct, may and do occur in rare instances in hospitals for the sane or insane, may be frankly admitted.
But such things are incidental to human relations of
every character. More insane persons are ill-treated,
injudiciously restrained, neglected and otherwise abused
while among friends in the family relation, than suffer
from similar treatment in the least reputable insane
hospital in America, proportionately considered.* But

---

* Dr. Crichton-Browne, English Visitor in Chancery, says, Parliamentary
Report, page 72: "It has fallen to my lot to admit hundreds of lunatics
covered with bruises, and with broken bones, or with other marks of injury
and violence. Frequently they are taken to the county asylums, tied up with
ropes and in strait waistcoats, and restrained in a way that never would be
tolerated in an asylum at the present time.

Q. Personal chastisement is not resorted to, I suppose? A. It is never
heard of in asylums. An attendant may lose his temper and commit violence upon a patient, but such a thing as deliberate chastisement is out of
question in asylums, although it does occur, I believe, amongst private cases
sometimes. One of my colleagues brought to the knowledge of the board a
case in which a birch rod was kept for the correction of a private lunatic.

Q. In those cases you mention in which marks were found upon lunatics, can such incidents be placed beyond the range of possibility or probability, in hospital administration, by the adoption of new methods? Welcome the day when such shall be devised. Sancho Panza's gratitude to "the man who invented sleep" was not greater than ours should be for such a consummation. But certain it is no such methods have as yet been suggested, much less put in practice. English methods, Scottish methods, Belgian methods, Gheel itself, with the canonized bones of St. Dymphna thrown in, have not accomplished so desirable an end.

The proposition of "American reformers" to convert the limited and responsible autocracy of present methods into an aristocracy of hospital officials of various grades, who, appointed by American methods, would become either more despotic and irresponsible by combining in a common interest, or disastrously weak and inefficient by dissensions and antagonism, does not promise well to comprehensive and considerate minds. It would be folly to attempt to govern insane men by such methods—not even by party caucus, and stump oratory of the most eloquent could it be done. Sane men—those who need to be governed, can not be well governed so. Insane men can not await cabinet consultations nor the possible deadlocks of conflicting differences of opinion. The greatest possible wisdom and liberality of government, is not incompatible with large discretionary power. The most arbitrary and ungenerous rule may be established and exercised by majorities, committees

---

that would not be from ordinary chastisement which was part of the system of the asylum, but from the unauthorized assault of an attendant? *A.* In those that were brought to the asylum the marks were due to assaults by relatives and friends. In those cases the marks of flogging have been discovered."

of safety, *vigilantes* and the like in the name of humanity and liberty. It is not the latent existence of
force in nature that is significant, but its applied activi-
ties. It is not the possession of power that character-
izes government, but the use which is made of it. And
it will be found, if closely scrutinized, that the reputation, characteristics and success of insane hospitals in
the United States and elsewhere, correspond to the
character, ability and attainment of their medical superintendents, and the manner in which they have been
sustained in authority by trustees and legislators, rather
than to the merits or demerits of any prescribed system of administration.*

Among those who are now most clamorous for struc-
tural and administrative reformation of American provision for the insane, there are persons who are not free
from suspicion that they are more interested in revolu-
tionizing present methods than they are in general
results. There are others, many, who are simply zeal-
ous and inconsiderate—men who, seeing but one corner
of a thing, are incapable of comprehending that there are
necessarily other corners which it would be worth while
to find out. The inference of hospital critics and reviewers, that managers and medical officers of American
institutions, are, with a few notable exceptions, selfish,
dishonest, criminal and despotic, simply because they

---

* "On examining closely the general condition of asylums, those are almost
always found to be best managed in which the physician is the superintendent one, and supreme—in which the committee of visitors act only
through him and with his advice—and in which the appointment and dis-
missal of all attendants are delegated to him ; and those are found to be
least satisfactory, in which the responsibility is divided—in which the committee of visitors or controlling board meddle in the internal management of
the institution, and direct themselves, or through other officers, any part of
it, appoint and dismiss attendants, or clip in any way the authority of the
medical superintendent." (Report on Lunatic Asylums by Frederic Norton
Manning, M. D., to Her Majesty's Colonial Secretary for New South Wales.)

have an opportunity to be so, "human nature being as it is," is as narrow-minded and malignant as the most orthodox believer in the dogma of "total depravity" or the devil himself, the arch-enemy of virtue and the human race could desire, and worthy only of the contempt of an enlightened people. Yet there are multitudes who have been and will be influenced by persistent and earnest assertion of inferences, no more accurate or philosophical; persons who are always ready to incline their ears to receive any imputation of wrong-doing on the part of others, especially such as may have become more prominent than themselves in any of the more reputable walks of life.

That the Superintendents of American Hospitals for the Insane should become conspicuous marks for constitutional detractors to expend their envious arrows on, is not a matter which should astonish the thoughtful. That they should be denounced as despots and obstructionists by the same class is not to be wondered at. Notwithstanding the fact that there are no officers in public service whose most trivial acts are so known and commented upon and so exposed to misconstruction and unfriendly criticism. Notwithstanding legislative and judicial investigations, industriously and sometimes malignantly prosecuted, have seldom failed to vindicate their general conduct. Notwithstanding they have kept pace with the progress of science and humanity wherever recognized, reserving only a certain self-respecting right of independent judgment of what is scientific and what is humane. Notwithstanding their readiness to conform these hospitals structurally and administratively to all modifications of conditions and circumstances which may affect hospital population, incident to natural causes; whether it be the gradual diminution of the use of mechanical restraints corresponding with the accumulation of chronic inmates, or the overflow of quiet, homeless lunatics no longer requiring hospital treatment, into detached buildings of less expensive character. Notwithstanding they are in their associated capacity less dogmatic, dictatorial, or limited by fixed ideas, constitution, creed or code, than any other organized society on earth. Notwithstanding, in their individual capacities, crippled as they have been and always will be, more or less, by the inevitable subordination of professional ideas, to the necessities of political or pecuniary exigencies, they have accomplished general results in their treatment of the insane, which compare favorably with the general results of the most vaunted hospitals and asylums of the old world. In their association they have always maintained the widest freedom of discussion, and have had before them in the thirty-five years of the existence of the Association all the problems, great and small, which concern the whole field of psychological medicine, and no adulations, threats or attacks have, or ever will swerve them from their course. Their records will show their work.

Compare, for example, the fact that the ratio of recoveries on the whole number of insane persons admitted to the Pennsylvaia Hospital for the Insane for forty years, ending with 1880, as reported by Dr. Kirkbride, "in whom," it may be said, if of any man, "there is no guile," has been forty-five per centum, with the fact that the ratio of recoveries, as reported by the honorable Commissioners in Lunacy, for 1880, on the whole number admitted to all of the public asylums and hospitals in England, idiot institutions excluded, for the year, was thirty-eight per centum.* Or, compare the results of thirty-eight years' operation of the

---

* *Journal Mental Science,* January, 1881.

asylum at Utica, from its opening to the end of 1880, showing a ratio of recoveries on the whole number admitted, of thirty-seven per centum, with the English results above quoted! A showing quite satisfactory when it is remembered that this exhibit of American results is drawn from a period of forty years, during which, if our critics and reviewers are to be believed, no progress has been made by Americans; while the English showing is from the operation of but one year, the last of thirty-five, since when English methods and practice have been declared by them as steadily progressing and improving!

But, lest some one might think this comparison limited and partial, compare the fact that the ratio of mortality on the average population in all of the English asylums and hospitals for the year 1880, as reported by the Lunacy Commissioners of England, [*Journal Mental Science*, January, 1881,] was nine and sixty-three one hundredths per centum, with the fact that the ratio of mortality for the same period, on the average population in the Pennsylvania hospital for the insane [Official Report, 1880] was seven and seventy-five one hundredths per centum, and the fact that the ratio of mortality for the same period in the Utica asylum was six and eighty-nine one hundredths per centum.

The uncharitableness of ignorance only would be illustrated by an attempt to draw conclusions from these facts derogatory to the English system of caring for the insane, or to institute invidious distinctions in favor of American hospitals. The facts are creditable to both English and American institutions. And we may frankly confess that which it would be presumptuous and arrogant to deny, that English asylums and hospitals and English methods of administration are-

the best possible, considered in relation to English characteristics, personal and institutional—while we should not hesitate to demand for American hospitals and methods, in the light of such results, a like respectful consideration. American intelligence can be trusted to find out and to appropriate whatever is useful or profitable in civilization, and to so far modify or reconstruct American institutions of whatever character, political, social, educational, or charitable, as to harmonize them with the necessities of any given time or combination of circumstances. The American people are neither obstructive nor obtuse to whatever is good, or advantageous—nor are they slow to act in the direction of their higher perceptions—but not even they can afford to fly in the face of established facts or to ignore the experience of the ages.

CINCINNATI SANITARIUM, June 6, 1881.

DISCUSSION.

Dr. Workman, following Dr. Everts, read a paper on "Some Points on the Management of American Institutions for the Insane."*

The Association then proceeded to discuss the papers read by Drs. Everts and Workman, and were called upon by the Vice President in turn as they sat in the room.

Dr. Bucke, of London, Ontario, said : Mr. President, I have listened to these two papers with as much pleasure, I think, as I have ever listened to any papers read in this Association, which is saying a great deal. I have very little indeed to say about them, but I just want to make one remark which is applicable to both papers. I· think that one of the great vices of the human mind is its tendency to what we may call finality. In every department of thought and life, and in every age there has always been an immense majority of the human race in any given state, or in any given country, who have thought that the end was reached. This remark is just as applicable to times of comparative darkness—of thousands or hundreds of years ago— as it is to-day, and a very little reflection would convince any person that the tendency is as little justified to-day as it was in the past.

In the care and treatment of the insane enormous advance has been made, even within the last few years, and if we go back hundreds of years the advance is so great that we can not estimate it. The inevitable tendency is to think that the work is done.

Now, although we can not see beyond where we are, it is just as certain that we are going to advance and go forward, as it is that the earth is going to continue to revolve around the sun. The direction in which we are going to advance, and the position towards which we are advancing, we can not say, but we should be very careful, I think, to condemn any suggestion tending forwards. I know even during my life that things are done— plans are carried out in asylums—that in my recollection would not have been thought possible, and the idea of which would have been hooted at. Even in my own asylum, I have 180 patients who are subject to no restraint, who go about as they please, who have all the privileges almost of sane people, and still they are just as insane as any other part of the population of my asylum. It would not have been thought possible, twenty or fifty years ago, to maintain lunatics in such a way. Not only is this true, but no evil has ever resulted from this increase of freedom, so that I am inclined to think more and more that the same freedom could be extended, although I might be very much afraid myself to extend it. Still I am satisfied that, although I may not do it, it will be done. I must say I very much prefer to see new ideas encouraged than to see them treated with levity, simply because they are new and untried. Of course it is very certain, as every one knows, that for every good idea advanced in any department of human life, there are a hundred very poor ones. At the same time I am inclined myself to look favorably upon every new idea, so far at least as to give it full consideration before discarding it, and to believe that we have not reached the end of our journey yet.

Dr. J. Z. GERHARD, of Harrisburg, Pa., said: I do not think I can let this opportunity pass without saying at least a few words. I was pleased with the remarks of the gentleman who just preceded me (Dr. Bucke). There was much in the papers read here this afternoon that I enjoyed. Although I speak as a very young member of this Association—and I hesitate to speak in this body, particularly in the presence of so many old members—yet I wish to add my views to those that were expressed by the speaker who preceded me. There is a feeling sometimes among men who are engaged in any special work that they are doing just right, that they have reached the highest point of excellence, and that there is no room for progress or advancement. Yet I believe that in the course of time (particularly with those who are young) we shall see many things differently from what we do now, and be able and willing to admit ideas that we now consider very absurd.

In the State from which I represent an institution, there is a feeling that something different should be done in connection with our hospitals. This feeling has manifested itself in such a strong manner that the organization of some hospitals has been changed to a certain extent. Efforts have been made at different meetings of our Legislature to change them still further. This desire for a change manifested itself very strongly in the last meeting of the Legislature, and there were very animated discussions on the organization of our hospitals. Radical changes have been made in two of the hospitals in Pennsylvania. Some men engaged in hospital work in the State are not in sympathy with them, others are, and mean to respect the sentiments thus expressed, to give them a fair chance with the hope also that they may be a success, and with the determination that they shall be a success.

Dr. T. M. FRANKLIN, of Blackwell's Island, N. Y., said: I can hardly resort to the same apology that Dr. Gerhard has offered in advancing his views here—that of extreme youth—but, perhaps I may say that, although a new member of this Association, I have been so long an interested observer of its workings and spirit, that neither of them is new to me. While a student, it was my privilege, as guest of Dr. Earle, of Bloomingdale, to be present at one of the sessions held by the now famous "original thirteen" who inaugurated this movement. I think it was the second meeting—the first having been held at Philadelphia.

Coming as I do from the State of New York, to which crimes against the insane of so many sorts have been attributed by those to whom allusion is made in one of the papers to which we have listened—belonging to the city of New York, and representing its female lunatic asylum—an institution habitually, semi-periodically, persistently and maliciously attacked, I can hardly maintain silence when the subject of these papers is under discussion.

We have a managing board, as you all know, politically composed, but, with its present organization and membership, I believe that, during the three years I have been connected with it, all has been done for the institution that the commissioners believed their peculiar and trying position would permit. As to visiting boards, inspecting boards and committees of sundry varieties, we have plenty; but we have, worse than all, people given to visitation and criticism, who belong to that "border-land" to which allusion has been made, and while we all know that "border-land" cases make us the most trouble, those nominally sane outsiders who are not under our control, sometimes behave still worse.

In regard to the question raised by Dr. Workman, as to the possibility of our being protected by boards, I am almost hopeless in this matter. I believe that years ago institutions for the insane under the control of individual States were not much influenced by politics. They are growing to be more and more so influenced. Of course the institutions of our large cities are very much so hampered.

As to our boards of management and the best methods of appointing them, I believe, sir, that any board composed of three or four reliable men (just enough to give variety to judgment) who have sufficient intelligence and education to learn how properly to investigate and oversee an institution—who are untrammeled—who are willing to give due time to the work, and will bring to it patient perseverance, who will intend to know what is doing and to become competent to pass judgment thereupon, will be perfectly able, no matter how appointed, to do all that is needful. In other words, innate reliability, acquired competency and individual independence, are the requisites. We know that the ordinary "committee of investigation" on management has not the practical knowledge requisite for getting at the state of an institution, and the true features of its conduct. We all know that such a body goes through an institution and comes out knowing very little of the internal workings of that institution. I venture to say that any member of this Association would feel, if he had an investigating board appointed by a senate or other authority go through his institution, that he was not properly inspected. If, then, he had any experienced member of this body come later, with power and determination to inspect his institution, he would think now I shall be thoroughly seen. That one man would shortly acquire such insight into your condition and management, as would astonish any committee and would do justice.

Boards and committees, as actually constituted, are sometimes hampered by political connections, through which they dare hardly break, or by aspirations of some sort which they do not wish to jeopardize. No such organization can be relied upon as "a breakwater" for the medical superintendent when attacked. I think the safety of a superintendent consists mainly in coercing his board of management into a familiarity with his doings, in making its members conversant with the details of daily movement, in taking them as it were into silent partnership in all work, and therefore into partial responsibility through knowledge. Then if he gets into trouble that board must either stand by him in his trouble, or prove recreant to its trust.

Dr. J. B. ANDREWS, of Buffalo, N. Y., said: I have but a few remarks to make upon the papers which have been read. The paper by Dr. Everts is an interesting one, though he has had to deal with what has become a somewhat trite subject, the criticisms upon asylum matters in this country by those who would occupy the rôle of reformers. These criticisms are of the most incoherent and impracticable character, and for this reason it is impossible to discuss them in a satisfactory manner. The Doctor has evidently labored under this difficulty.

Fault is found with the lunacy laws and the details of their administration, with the conduct of the external and internal affairs of institutions, and with those who are intrusted with their charge. In short, nothing is right or worthy of commendation, and the most radical changes are demanded. Such wholesale criticisms are neither right nor reasonable, and those who make them seem actuated by a spirit of destructiveness, and a determination to overthrow everything which has grown up as the result of practical experience. They are founded largely upon loose, and sometimes false statements of comparisons, and upon specious reasoning which takes the place of knowledge, while the unprovoked attacks upon individuals place them beyond the limits which entitle them to any reply.

Dr. H. P. MATHEWSON, of Lincoln, Nebraska, said: I was desirous of meeting with this society, and have been gratified by the taking up of this question, which is a very interesting one. It appears to me that the successful management of the insane must depend largely upon the individual capacity of managers themselves—that person who is sufficiently vigilant to take up each case and treat that case as it needs, will best succeed. If we could lay down rules for the treatment of the insane, it might be different; but we may as well expect to lay down rules for everything else in the way of treatment. I do not suppose we are going to find anything more than general rules for the management and treatment of all our cases. If we had a specific for all diseases, the practice of medicine would be very easy. So in the management of insane, if we had a specific treatment, the greatest novice in the world could succeed. My knowledge of the treatment of the insane certainly is limited, but I have learned that we can not treat the insane all alike. We have to treat them as individual cases.

I was very much interested in the paper of Dr. Everts. Of course I have seen through the papers and in various ways noticed the large number of persons in New York, who are agitating a different treatment and management of the insane. I know some of the leaders, and I am confident that they know as little about it as an equal number of inexperienced persons upon any other subject. I do not believe they are actuated by honest motives, although I may be wrong about that. But one thing we may do well to consider, and that is, the proposition that reform "generally comes from the outside," and we ought to be willing to accept the situation. All suggestions coming honestly and conscientiously, we ought to take in good faith.

For my own part, I do not suppose that persons not accustomed to the management of the insane are going to learn all about it by theory. It must come mostly from practice and observation. The person who is determined to be vigilant and cautious, is most likely to best succeed. My impression is, that there is an immense amount to be learned in the care of insane people. We do not have to look back far to see improvements and reform in the care of the insane. Doubtless there is a large amount to be done in that direction, and I think we ought to go slowly in our criticisms in regard to these suggestions.

I am glad to meet with this Association, and to listen to the comparing of different views and facts. I did not come expecting that I should add anything, or even to suggest anything that would be of use or value, but I am glad to hear every man's views in this society. Every man is strange to me. There is not one person here that I have ever seen before; but I am very glad to see you, gentlemen, and to make your acquaintance.

Dr. A. M. FAUNTLEROY, of Staunton, Va., said: I have but little to say beyond the expression of the pleasure with which I listened to the reading of the *critique* by Dr. Everts. It is an admirable and biting satire upon the conduct of those self-constituted guardians of the insane, whose main business in life seems to be that of carping or fault-finding with asylum management. Doubtlessly we shall always have trouble as long as there remains one of that class of microscopic philanthropists whose " principal focal distance " rarely ever falls within the " visual field " of their *own concerns.* If any man takes an asylum, expecting it to be " a bed of roses," he is very much mistaken. And the only course which promises satisfaction to an asylum official, is to be found in the conscientious and persistent efforts to secure for those who are the tender objects of his solicitude and care, all the means which enlightened experience has shown to be most promotive of the interests and welfare of the insane.

In the proud consciousness of duty fulfilled, there lies capsulate the true psychological antidote to the annoyances which may never cease to arise this side of the advent of the millennium.

Dr. A. P. REID, of Halifax, Nova Scotia, said: I prefer to listen rather than talk in these discussions. There is a pleasure in listening to the different gentlemen giving their experiences of asylum management, or on any subject bearing on the treatment of insanity. It appears to me that in thirty or forty years at farthest, we have the largest portion of this continent supplied with buildings established for the care of the insane, and that we have reached so near perfection as to have but little fault found with the management of these institutions, is cause for self-congratulation. I do not know that we could get any other political machine to run as satisfactorily, because asylums for the insane must be considered more or less (if not all) under governmental supervision. It appears to me that we are in a state of improvement. Insane asylums have greatly progressed until now they can well be called "hospitals for the insane." I do not believe we will reach the highest success in hospital treatment until we get further towards the cure of mental diseases.

I do not suppose that anything causes so much alarm to outsiders as the so-called "restraints." Many, from ignorance, appear to act on the assumption that superintendents of hospitals for the insane are not governed by feelings common to the race of humanity, whereas, the principles guiding the management of every asylum I have ever visited, have been how much liberty and pleasure can be given to the insane. They desire to give all that is possible, having a due regard to the patient's benefit. I feel quite confident that it would be well for the public to know what superintendents aim at. The business and pleasure of every superintendent is to give every patient all the liberty possible, consistent with proper care and cure.

Dr. WM. B. GOLDSMITH, of Danvers, Mass. I only wish to state with reference to Dr. Workman's paper that I entirely agree with him as to the value of an expert supervisory board in the care of the insane. I do not think it would materially change the better class of asylums in the United States. In them the inspection of such a board would probably be largely a matter of form, as it is in institutions of a similar class elsewhere, but I think it would aid in securing a more uniformly good care for the insane, and render it more difficult for institutions to fall behind, or never reach a fair grade of excellence as they may now do in the States without general professional notice. I also think that it would be a protection to superintendents, and that it could fulfill most important duties in cases of patients possessed of property, and in rendering a variety of provision for the insane safer. There are many instances where the friends or guardians of patients have great difficulty in determining how they had best plan and provide for their charges, and whether they receive a fair equivalent for their outlay. There are also cases where a proper amount of the patient's property is not expended on their care. In these matters I think expert authorities should advise or decide.

Their oversight is also important in rendering a variety of provision for the insane safer. Without it I regard much variety of provision entirely unsafe, for there is no security for good treatment in private dwellings or asylums unless the amount of money involved is sufficient to secure the services of a humane and cultivated man, who has social standing and professional reputational station. With supervision I think the private home treatment admirable in many cases, without it I think it is to be condemned. I do not know whether Dr. Workman appreciates the force of one point he made as fully as I do. That is the difficulty of securing competent inspectors or commissioners in the States.

Though the appointment of a properly constituted board meets my approval, I regard the appointment of one improperly constituted as worse than useless, and the exercise of such authority without knowledge as very bad. In many of our States, at present, I think it would be found impossible to secure competent men to take the field. It is not a position in which a young man should win his spurs, but one that requires the experienced and judicial mind of mature age, and a proper candidate usually occupies a more stable position with higher salary than often goes with such appointments when our State legislatures govern them. I think this difficulty the great one in the United States, but the plan is good.

Dr. STRONG. I think it is obvious that we can not conclude this discussion at the present sitting, and I would, therefore, suggest a recess until 8 o'clock.

Dr. GUNDRY. I move to adjourn the discussion until to-morrow morning. I should like to take part in the discussion, but I can not do so this evening.

On motion, the Association adjourned to 9 A. M., Wednesday, June 15.

JUNE 15, 1881.

The Association was called to order at 10 A. M., by Dr. Callender.

The minutes of the proceedings of yesterday were read and approved.

The Secretary read a letter from Dr. T. J. Mitchell, of Mississippi, expressive of his regret at his inability to attend this meeting.

Dr. CALLENDER. On adjourning yesterday the Association had under consideration and for discussion the papers read by Drs. Everts and Workman, and Dr. Hughes was about to take the floor.

Dr. CHARLES H. HUGHES, of St. Louis, said: I have been a member of this Association for a number of years, and have been a constant observer of its work. Formerly I looked at the work of this Association from the inside of an asylum. I have been able, during the last seven years, to take an outside view of its workings, and I must say that my observation of the work of this body, as referred to in the paper of Dr. Everts, has been as satisfactory to me, viewing it from the outside, as it did when I viewed it as an asylum superintendent. I have contributed my own observation in a practical way, to a verification of most of the propositions which have from time to time been promulgated by this body, and I have found them to bear the test of experience. In fact, it does not occur to my memory that any similar number of propositions that have ever been made by any medical body, so long existent as this one has been, has been enabled so well to stand the test of time.

Now, there are two ways of viewing the subject of insanity and its relations. Metaphysical conceptions—theoretical opinions of what insanity ought to be, and of what ought to be done with the insane, are generally the first that present themselves to the mind of a medical man when his attention is turned to the subject. Theoretical conceptions of what insanity ought seemingly to be, frequently lead gentlemen to the formation of opinions as to its management and treatment very much at variance with the suggestions of actual experience.

Doubtless it has occurred to many a member of this Association that, in the beginning of his career upon taking charge of an institution for the insane, he has had theoretical conceptions of what insanity was, and formed conclusions based upon those theoretical conceptions, as to how the insane ought to be managed. And it is in the experience of every member of this Association, that observation of the insane—familiar intercourse with them—connected with those influences which have to do with their welfare, with legislation and boards of management—has led each and all of us to conclusions with regard to their management different from those which were held upon entering the special practical study of mental aberration.

This Association needs no defence, and it never would have occurred to me to write a paper in defence of the practical propositions of this body, because they are the formulated convictions of experience. I do not understand that the paper of Dr. Everts has been offered for that purpose. The point of the paper, that this Association has not been obstructive or retrogressive, or not progressive, certainly needs no defence. We need but look at the history of insanity in this country during the past half a century and compare the present ameliorated condition of the insane with their past—which has been the work of this Association and the work of government through them—for a historical proof of the good work that has been done by and through this body. Errors have been committed by architects, adornments have been added to buildings which have never been suggested by this body, expenditures have been made not warranted by any of the propositions of this Association, and other errors of omission and commission have been committed for which we are not at all responsible.

Gentlemen, outside of the specialty, are accustomed to point with commendable pride to the heroism of medical men in times past, to the spectacle of Vesalius, for example, making the first human dissection at a time, and in an age, when it required courage to face a frowning world. Triumph over adverse public opinion has added no greater laurels to the brow of victorious and progressive medicine than that sublime spectacle which took place in the dungeon cells of the Bicêtre, when our own Pinel, in the face of opposition equally as great, struck the shackles from the lunatics there confined and recognized those insane persons as friends and brothers, casting to the winds the theoretical dogma that they were fiends incarnate. This was the work of psychiatry and it was the work of our profession. It was the work done inside of asylums. There is where it began, inside of the asylum circles, and where it has resulted in benefit to the race. It was the beginning of that reform in psychiatry, that practical and beneficent form which has been going on from the days of Pinel to the present time within the asylums.

The first impression that I received from my intercourse with members of this Association in official capacity, was that of their earnestness in behalf of the insane, and subsequent repeated attendance upon the meetings of the Association and visiting of institutions throughout the country impressed me with the fact, that if ever there was a set of men alive to the truest interests of the insane it was the superintendents of the American hospitals. The presence of this body of men was always an inspiration, and

I never went among the members of this Association, either as superintendent of an asylum, or since, that I did not acquire an enlarged conception of the rights of the insane which I had never thought of or heard of outside. If there has been a body in existence which has kept constantly in view the rights of the insane, it has been this body, and it is that subject which occupies the attention of all of us—the rights of the insane. Their right to the largest liberty compatible with their welfare, and that higher right than liberty, which, if they could speak as others speak, they would demand of us the right to that scientifically regulated restraint which conduces to their speediest possible restoration to the usefulness of rational life, and any men, or any body of men, who are regardless of this right, inflict upon the insane—these helpless wards of those who are more fortunate than they—a wrong far greater than the deprivation of liberty.

One could not discuss the propositions of these papers without exhausting much more time than the papers themselves occupied. The points of Dr. Workman's paper in the main were points upon which this Association is committed as the detrimental influence of frequent rotations in office. Political changes in medical officers of hospitals for the insane conflict so sadly and so seriously with the rights of the insane that the fact needs but to be mentioned to be condemned, because if there is any one right above another that the insane would demand of us, could they speak as we speak, it is that in the days of their calamity they might receive from us, or they might receive from those States, which assume to take charge of them in their affliction when they can not care for themselves, that ministering medical care which can only come from experience and observation, and when asylum physicians are changed, as they are in some of the States of this Union every two years, it is a farce and a travesty on justice to say that the insane man, who is a ward of such a State, is accorded his rights when he has to receive only such medical attention. The principle of the proper treatment of insanity is somewhat akin to the increased experience and skill required to navigate a ship, where laws are framed for the purpose of securing life, personal safety, not at the hands of novices but experienced seamen. How much more important is it that States should be particular to see and provide that skill and experience should be furnished to the hospitals for the insane, and that the tenure of office of medical officers of asylums should not be subjected to those changes which are dependent upon party exigencies.

In regard to the question of inspectors, there can be no objection to an inspection *per se* in stable governments like Great Britain, not subject to those periodical changes which sweep biennially and quadrennially over our States and our country, where there would be great danger in having one more asylum officer added to this large number which are subject to political change. I have no objection to medical inspectors of asylums, if they are the right kind of men. There can be no valid objection to having institutions inspected by men of experience. This Association has no objection to anything that promises to ameliorate the condition and welfare of the insane. It has been the habitual thought of almost all the members of this body, so far as I have been able to glean it, that if a body of five or seven or nine men in a single State of this Union, having but two or three asylums to look after, and having but one under their own immediate eye, could not be selected by the Governor, by and with the advice and consent of the Senate, of sufficient probity and character to manage the affairs of an asylum, it would be exceedingly difficult to make matters much better by adding one more. The objection is not to the system of inspection, the objection is to the probable inexperience and instability of the inspectorship that would be established.

A system of inspection may be a farce under one manner of conducting it and in one country, and work most admirably in another. The very same inspector of the hospitals for the insane who inspected these asylums, when we were here ten years ago, is the very same gentleman who greets us here to-day, and I am sure we are all glad to welcome him and glad to know that the asylums of this province have an inspector whose tenure of office does not depend upon the political changes of ephemeral political parties. How would it be with us? How many Langmuirs should we see in our States for a single decade, under our present vicious system of rotation in office and spoils to the political victors? It would be perilous to the general welfare of our insane to advocate a general inspector for the insane, unless we could secure stability in office and be assured of adequate qualifications on the part of the inspector.

There are a large number of other points in these interesting papers which will be covered by the other gentlemen. I am sure, gentlemen, I have occupied more than my share of the time.

Dr. A. E. Macdonald. I was not permitted the pleasure of listening to Dr. Workman's paper yesterday. As regards the paper of Dr. Everts, there is but a single point upon which I desire to speak to the Association. As I understand the Doctor, he intimated an opinion that perhaps more should have been done by members of the Association residing in New York and its vicinity, in the way of answering the attacks upon asylum management throughout the country, for the reason that the persons making such attacks were for the most part resident in New York. As a representative of the asylum which is perhaps closer than any other to the body of gentlemen who have been so industriously attacking these institutions, I will say that I have not deemed it necessary to meet them in their attacks in any way, except when brought before some legally constituted body.

First of all, I beg to remind you that we are pretty well acquainted with the gentlemen who make these attacks. We know just who they are and what they wish to attain, and the weight they have in the communities in which they reside. If they have more weight with gentlemen in other localities, it comes only from that enchantment which distance always lends.

The attacks, as you are all aware, originated in a body in New York, called the "Neurological Society," and from a paper read there some years ago, this great "reform" has spread. It was my privilege to have been a member of that society previous to that attack; as it was also my privilege immediately thereafter to resign. I was present at the meeting at which this paper was read.

In order that you may have some idea of the importance and numerical strength of that society, I will tell you that there were just thirteen persons in the room, at least three of whom were not members of the society; and of whom others, including myself, were not entirely in sympathy with the views of that paper. In fact, when it became necessary for the chairman to make the appointment of a committee of three to carry out the objects of the paper, he named one gentleman who got up and said he could not very well serve, as he did not belong to the society.

There are, Mr. President, some four thousand physicians in New York and the surrounding cities. I think you can count upon the fingers, perhaps of one hand, the members of the profession who have taken any active part in this crusade; and of those whom you can count, you may judge something of their bias and of their importance when I tell you that one of them, the vice president of this august body of which I have spoken, was a rejected applicant for place at half a dozen asylums; who consequently formed the conclusion that there was something rotten within these asylums that he should reform. If any member thinks it desirable to silence him, he might offer him a position.

Another, of equally exalted rank, revealed a possible personal interest when he told a gentleman, whose signature he solicited, that the result of the movement might be to secure a position in an asylum for himself; and of the few who remain two or three are practitioners who treat the insane at their own homes, and who are, not unnaturally, strong advocates for home treatment for the insane.

Any agitation regarding the management of insane asylums which begets a temporary fear or distrust upon the part of those who have insane relatives, and a consequent retention of the latter at their homes, brings so much grist to the mills of these gentlemen. I do not, for one, propose to constitute myself an advertising bureau in their service.

It is true that the persons of whom I have spoken, sensible of their own want of standing with the community, have, by one device and another, attracted to their standard a few whom they thought capable of strengthening their position, and naturally these accessions have been less from the ranks of their own profession, where they are known, than from among the laity.

Perhaps the most prominent of their allies, thus gained, is Mr. Dorman B. Eaton, to whom Dr. Everts has in his paper particularly referred. I shall tell you a little incident in regard to that gentleman's attacks upon the asylums, and leave Dr. Everts and yourselves to judge what force should attach to his utterances, and how much is to be gained by trying to meet them in a fair and manly way. I am not personally acquainted with Mr. Eaton, nor have I, to my knowledge, ever seen him; but I am told that he is a gentleman, who having in his younger days performed valuable public service, has reached now an age and a frame of mind when he takes upon himself the rôle of a common scold, and generally behaves as though the whole world had been laid at his feet with the injunction—"O, reform it altogether."

There had been a hearing before a committee of the State Senate, appointed to investigate the management of insane asylums, and an employé of the Ward's Island Asylum, who had been in the service long before I assumed charge, saw fit to make a comparison between the management at the time of his appointment and of his testimony. This comparison happened to be complimentary to the present management, and he incidentally cited a very undesirable condition of affairs as existing a number of years before, but now entirely abolished. Now this was not at all the material that Mr. Eaton and his *confrères* wanted; according to them, there was no improvement and nothing that was not bad— so if Mr. Eaton had read the testimony aright, he would doubtless have quietly ignored it, but by some singular mistake or accident, or lapse of memory or something, for of course Mr. Eaton would not willfully distort or garble, the testimony was so transformed that it was made to come from myself instead of the employé, to apply to the period of my own administration instead of that of a remote predecessor, and so became very fair evidence in favor of the urgent need of reform, and consequently such as Mr. Dorman B. Eaton could use without affecting his conscientious scruples against saying anything at all favorable to the asylums or their officers.

I was foolish enough to do upon that one occasion what Dr. Everts suggests might perhaps be oftener done—to meet the attack in a less formal way than simply before legally constituted bodies. I shall not do it again; and I leave you to judge whether or no I am right. I thought that Mr. Eaton differed from his associates sufficiently to make an appeal to his sense of justice and fair play practicable, and I wrote to him as follows, forwarding my letter only after submitting it to the commissioners of my department for their approval:

New York, April 16, 1881.

Dorman B. Eaton, Esq.:

My Dear Sir: I saw, yesterday, for the first time, an article in the *North American Review* for last month, over your signature, in which the following paragraph occurs:

"Only last week the present Superintendent of the Ward's Island Asylum gave this testimony before the committee just referred to: 'When I came on the Island, I was more afraid of the keepers than the lunatics. The keepers were mostly shoulder-hitters, and they made a regular slaughter-house of the place.'"

In view of the possible existence in the peculiar code of asylum assailants of some Statute of Limitations under which a falsehood becomes equivalent to the truth if uncontradicted for a certain period, will you permit "the present Superintendent of the Ward's Island Asylum" to say to you that neither "last week" nor at any other time, neither "before the committee just referred to" (that of the State Senate) nor in any other presence, did he use the words which you put into his mouth, or any others conveying in the remotest degree the same meaning, actual or colorable, express or implied; and that what was said of this nature was by quite a different person and with reference to quite a different period. I do not assert or assume that the falsehood is your own; certain persons for certain personal reasons, have put in circulation malicious fabrications regarding the management of insane asylums, and feeling that their own names would rather discredit than strengthen their charges, they have sought the weight of other and better names, whose owners have been prejudicial enough or weak enough to lend them without due investigation. It has been in some such way as this, probably, that you have been led to father a deliberate and ingenious misstatement. I may be mistaken, but it seems to me that a moral obligation rests upon the man who is anxious to say hard things of another, to first make sure that they are true things as well as hard, and when he avoids obvious and accessible means of enquiry, it appears as though he were too anxious to say the hard things to be willing to run the risk of learning that they are untrue.

The asylum on Ward's Island is within an hour's journey of your office, and access to it, and ample opportunity of examining it, could have been obtained at any time. They are still available, and though you will scarcely, after this letter, view the asylum with any lessening of the prejudice which you have so plainly shown, I do not doubt that you will be forced to the conviction, though not perhaps to the admission, that much else that you have said is, as regards it, as unfounded as the particular assertion which I have herein corrected.

Your obedient servant,
A. E. MACDONALD,
Medical Superintendent.

Mr. Eaton's answer was as follows:

2 EAST TWENTY-NINTH STREET,
NEW YORK, April 20, 1881.

My Dear Sir: Yours of the 16th was received last evening. I am never willing to do any man injustice, and shall always be glad to make redress for any wrong I may have inadvertently done. The language referred to by you was reported as a part of the testimony in a morning journal, (I am almost certain it was the *Times*), of the day after it was taken. I had interviews with two of the Senate Committee, and satisfied myself that it was reliable. There was wish to say any hard thing. (So in the letter. Mr.

Eaton probably meant to say "there was *no* wish, &c.," but strict accuracy is perhaps subserved by the omission.)

Going to the Island would not show me what was said before the committee surely. I regret that I have not kept the paper; but I am certain the language to be there given and I never saw any correction of it, though I am a regular reader of the *Times*.

It is very likely the testimony was given by the out-warden instead of the superintendent, (since I do not question your declarations), and that I or the editor may have inadvertently attributed it to the wrong official.

If you have suffered injustice, in that particular, which I can remedy, I shall be glad to do so, as you may suggest.

I then believed, as I now do, though only on the basis of general information, that the administration of the asylum had improved under your charge.

My first draft, I think, directly suggested that fact, but it was not material to state, and the facts I had at hand did not warrant a volunteer statement to that effect.

If you will look a little more calmly at what I did say, you will see that it carries a strong inference for improvement. No man can read it without the idea that things are now better, and that the writer of the article was willing that inference should be drawn. Hoping, therefore, you may think better of my motives and of my care in writing, I am,

Your obedient servant,

To Dr. Macdonald.   D. B. EATON.

I at once carefully examined again all the newspaper accounts of the committee's investigation, and found that in no one of them was the testimony quoted ascribed to me, and that the *Times* was especially far from doing so, as it gave the name of the witness in full more than once, "Cyrus Pearsall" and "A. E. Macdonald" ought not to be absolutely indistinguishable.

Two months have passed, and I have seen no outward manifestation of the spirit of unwillingness to do any man injustice, of which Mr. Dorman B. Eaton eloquently writes—nor has he accepted my invitation to visit the asylum, though he has found time to go to one more remote—that at Flatbush, and to adopt and disseminate the cheerful little fiction regarding it as to the total abolition of restraint apparatus. So that I am considerably strengthened in my belief that there is nothing to be gained by following our accusers into places where we are not bound to meet them, and where ordinary rules of justice and decency do not prevail.

When they have had the temerity to assail us where we could properly reply, we have met them very promptly, and I think very conclusively. Two years ago they were given the amplest opportunity of substantiating their accusations before a Senate Committee, and they entirely failed and drew upon themselves a scathing rebuke from the committee, upon which they immediately turned round and abused *it.* Another committee has been sitting during the past winter, and has asked leave to defer its report for another year, so that at least it can not have found need for immediate and radical reform.

I am, for myself, content to leave matters with such committees, and to such and other legitimate means of enquiry and defence. To follow our accusers into the newspapers and elsewhere is to give them what they most desire—notoriety, recognition. They are like the man who thought he had gained in social standing because he had been kicked by George the Fourth.

You may judge of the importance that is attached to these gentlemen, and their assertions in the community where they are best known, by seeing what they have accomplished. If they have had any weight it has been in places where they are not known—in Wisconsin or Pennsylvania, not in New York. For one I certainly do not admit that it is incumbent upon us to leave the positions to which the public has elevated us, and to go down to meet every Tom, Dick and Harry who chooses to throw mud at us.

Dr. J. STRONG, of Cleveland, Ohio, said: Dr. Macdonald has nearly spoiled what I designed to say on this question. I had supposed that Mr. Dorman B. Eaton was a man of more consequence and sense than he is willing to concede to him. The Doctor has personal knowledge of the man, while I have only impressions of him which I have gathered from his writings. Mr. Eaton is certainly a man of considerable prestige in some respects. He was selected by the general government, a few years ago, as one of a committee to examine into, and, report upon a plan to reform and reorganize the civil service of the United States.

It has been claimed here that the article of Mr. Eaton on the " Despotism of Superintendents of Asylums for the Insane " refers principally to those in the State of New York. Now there happen to be several asylums for the insane in this country outside of the State of New York. He chose a literary publication of large circulation and wide reputation, as an instrument of attack on the

American system of treating the insane, generally accompanied with unworthy and untruthful thrusts at superintendents of our insane asylums in particular. Poison does not always antidote itself. I do not believe that such a tirade, although to some the *animus* of the writer may be apparent, should be passed by unnoticed. When the article in the *North American Review* first appeared, I could but look upon it as one of those literary assaults that was connived in blissful ignorance of the subject discussed, strongly tinged with a fanatical hue, and couched in the language of charlatanism. I rejoice that Dr. Everts has pricked the bubble and exposed the hollowness of the article in question. We must remember that almost everybody reads now-a-days, and it is but just and fair that both sides should be presented to the reading public; that the antidote should follow the poison, and in this particular instance Dr. Everts has most effectually done so, and I thank him for it.

Now these efforts on the part of pseudo-reformers, as previously remarked, do not always antidote themselves. They do, to a certain extent, exert an unwholesome influence on the public mind. They tend to weaken the public faith in our asylums, and thereby impair their usefulness. The dissemination of such views as those contained in the article of Mr. Eaton, has the effect to strengthen prejudice in the minds of those who are already too prone to indulge in unfounded reflections, and uncharitable feelings toward asylums. The true philanthropist will do all in his power to enlighten the public mind in relation to the high and holy mission of our asylums, and will use his utmost endeavors to neutralize and correct tendencies to erroneous opinions held in regard to them.

The charlatan on the other hand, too frequently, as in the present instance, aims to use popular prejudice and credulity to promote and carry forward his mischievous work. As a practical illustration of the evil which flows from these wicked tirades against asylums—based sometimes on ignorance and sometimes on malice—let me refer to the very frequent hesitation of friends of the insane to send the latter early to an asylum. Now whatever tends to weaken public confidence in asylums, strengthens this feeling of hesitation of friends of the insane to place the latter promptly under asylum treatment which may offer the only means of recovery. I need not stop here to dwell upon the priceless advantages of early asylum treatment. I desire rather to refer to those obstacles which stand in the way of early treatment, and hint at the responsibility of those who are instrumental in creating such obstacles.

Dr. GUNDRY. Mr. President, I did not have the pleasure of hearing the paper of my friend, Dr. Everts, and I shall not allude to it at all in what I have to say, except in regard to one or two things said since. I heard Dr. Workman's paper, and to that I briefly address myself. I am very thoroughly of the views there expressed, and possibly, with one exception, I might adopt them as my own. I believe that the best means of reform is to let the light into every place. However much it may cause a temporary depression in our case, it will eventually result in a greater and more favorable movement in our behalf. All advance movements are met with walls of stone before the great asylums themselves. We do not make progress in this. We are, by straight lines or by curves, going backwards, and I recently overheard an intelligent friend make a remark to this effect. It is the one great obstacle in our profession. He had only just been appointed to an asylum. It is only from the fact of going out and looking in, that we get the views of others, and it was this fact that enabled him to make this expression.

All reform in asylums came over to the United States through the unobtrusive action of Tuke, and it is to Tuke, really, that we owe all the improvements in management which have come down to us. It has simply been improving and developing the germinal seed that he deposited. It is all very well to recognize the great claims of Pinel and others, but we can not avoid recognizing the efforts of the family of Tukes. They were called to them by certain language of a persistent member before the House of Commons. So it will not do to argue that the efficacious reforms came from within, when, in fact, the greatest reforms have come from without.

The one point which I wish to speak mostly to, of the subjects to which Dr. Workman alluded, is the necessity of governmental inspection. Now, do not be carried away with fears. First, I see the governmental inspector present, and I shall use the liberty of speaking of him as I would not if he were absent. The inspectorship in Canada is not that which is required by our hospitals, because the inspector of hospitals here has also the management combined in the same person. That is an essential difference. The inspector of Canadian institutions is the substitute of the boards of management throughout the United States. It is not as in Ohio, where each institution is under a separate board of trustees. Now, if they were all transferred to one board, that board stands in the same relation that the inspector of asylums and institutions does in Canada. In addition to that, they were subordinate and responsible to the people. By laws, or some cabinet procedure, he is responsible to the State. I believe that is a fair statement. The plan has worked well, and it was claimed, yesterday, that it enabled them, and no doubt it does enable them, to be free from certain political influences, and to be rid of a great many anomalies that are found in some United States institutions. If the Canadian institutions are free from all such embarrassments, they are to be congratulated that they have had the small pox of politics; but having got through, it is hardly fair to fire at us, who are working through it with the virus among us. Some of them will hardly acknowledge that they have had it, but I will show them that they have, to my certain knowledge. But the point I wish to speak upon, is governmental inspection. By governmental, I mean rising from the government. That is the most certain to be popular in this region. What I wish to say is just this. Some boards are constituted with the idea of prominency, having no connection with the management of the institution, having no power to alter errors of judgment, and no power to inspect, rigidly, every inmate in the institution, or the inmate of every family who has insane there, not having the right to report, or the right to remedy an abuse which exists, by bringing it before the notice of the party or parties who have the authority or power to remedy it. Of course, there are instances where they should have no power in themselves.

Now, I contend that a board properly constituted of men of business experience, medicine and law combined, of such character as would command the respect of all the good citizens of the State, would stand as a bulwark between the patients and the public. It would be a source of protection, really, for the superintendents. The first protection is from that called political influence. I amused myself, when the gentleman was speaking, by recounting, in my memory, all the names of the gentlemen, in the course of my career, who have served as superintendents of hospitals in one State. I found that twenty-seven superintendents have served in the five hospitals of one State, during the time I have been connected with this specialty; that there are now living, thirteen superintendents.

Dr. Gray. Name the State.

Dr. Gundry. No, sir. I am not going to name anything—that there are thirteen ex-superintendents now living of one State who have been in active service. I beg pardon there are fourteen ex-superintendents on the roll. In one case the board of trustees deliberately said that "the reason we succeed you in the office of superintendent, which we do to-day, is that in this State it has been the custom of both parties to fill these positions with persons in harmony with the political party in power," and closing with the statement that "we are most sincerely your friends and well-wishers," etc.

Now that affects one man, but the principle affects all men. What protection would that be to the man who succeeded the man who was the recipient of that letter? If all the best men in the world came, they have to displace the man who had served the State long and faithfully. That is a general statement. Now in order to make up a statement that the State has suffered no loss, these men, personal friends of the gentleman to whom they wrote the letter, must necessarily be biased in favor of the man whom they had put in the position; and therefore any controversy arising, they would be utterly powerless to stem the tide of public opinion and be bound by a course proper and right. They would be biased to a certain extent.

Take another case. Suppose trustees, and remember that it is not in every State that trustees of the highest character, both morally and pecuniarily, are always obtained, that in some States we get men who are engaged in the business of making money, etc., and not unfrequently bring them from pursuits which make it desirable for them that they should be brought in connection with the institution for the opportunities afforded. Now suppose a majority of such trustees with a friend as superintendent, whereby on the one hand you could have the trustees, and on the other the laws carried out and respected by the chief medical officer, would it be surprising to generate in the minds of such men a prejudice against this person with whom they are mingling, or that the other trustees could not devise a plan by which that man could be got rid of? Then if a change is made what protection is there to the person who succeeds? There is none I am sorry to say.

A gentleman, one of our body, was unfortunate enough to be connected politically with a very aspiring and able man. That gentleman unfortunately received the votes of a body for a very high office, for which another gentleman holding the executive department was an aspirant. It so happened that living in the same State was an old gentleman who had long desired and panted for the place which this man had long occupied in the asylum. It also so happened that this old man had some political influence, and he had worked it up for this gentleman who was defeated for this high position in the national councils. And presto, things changed. A vacancy occurred in the board of trustees, and it was filled up so that the gentleman who had not failed in his efforts for his friend, so far as the high position was concerned, was displaced by the gentleman who worked for the unsuccessful competitor. What help to the board can such a man be, or to those who put him there? By and by he is shriveled and cast aside as asleep and worthless. I am not going to attack any person, I am leaving out names, but I stand here personally responsible for every statement I make.

Of course all I am talking about refers principally to State institutions. There is a class of incorporated institutions also which, in my opinion, requires the same supervision and the same power to manage as any State institution of the country. There are but two institutions that I will refer to that I make an exception of, the Pennsylvania Hospital for the Insane in Philadelphia, under the care of Dr. Kirkbride, and the Friends' Asylum. They are so intimately connected with a large and influential body of religious men, and their boards are so largely composed of the best of that honorable sect, that really the society itself stands in a certain degree as a wall around them; and there is a consciousness of the fact that nothing irregular or wrong in these institutions could be kept one moment, if suspected or thought of, by the members of that body, without being discovered and corrected; and hence these institutions have, as a wall of fire, that which protects them against any vile imaginings that may be carried among good thinking people. What the Society of Friends have and enjoy is a power which I think a State board of inspectors ought to have, and we have more necessity for it than the Society of Friends. The management that they have, the power and the possibility of protection, is what I contend for in the breast of the inspector in every State in our Union. I personally would greatly prefer a national board, but I am well aware that it would be impossible for one board to inspect all properly, and that it would be necessary to have a number of boards, to have the work done properly and thoroughly, remembering that in every institution the insane ought to be looked after, and properly treated, fed and cared for. Then there are private institutions, and persons treated at the homes of others, and in poor-houses persons away from the observation of society, who should come under the protection of such a board as I speak of. I am aware that it will add to the expense, but it will add to the protection of the insane, and it will add greatly to the protection of those who have the care of the insane in our institutions.

Now, there are certain objections, of course, to all this. It may be urged that "the stream can not rise higher than its source," that in new countries and new conditions of society, you will not be able to get that which you have in some of the old societies and communities. Nevertheless—and this is frequently answered and frequently charged—it is surprising how the back is fitted to the burden, and how people who at first are thought inadequate to the position or to the office, actually do far more in practice, and do their duty more freely than we could expect. In these new States we would have a number with the interests of society at heart—men who would soon become accustomed to their duties, and do them just as thoroughly as the most highly educated people of this country. When we are apprehensive of danger of mistakes to be made by others, it is just as well to look and see if we have not made some of the same color, and whether we have not produced some of the same feeling that we censure.

None of us are agreed, probably, as to the mode in which reform should be carried out, or developed, as some choose to call it, or how it should be carried out in our institutions. Some have larger liberty than others. Each may have his individual opinion, and each is entitled to a respectful consideration of that opinion. We, as you know, are a staid and selfish race. We have no organ to represent us, or we are represented by an organ which is owned and controlled by one institution. That journal, being the only journal published, until recently, is, to some extent, considered the organ of the Association. It unfortunately happens that it has assailants, and, therefore, we have the anomaly, how it comes that Utica politics should assume such prominence, both in asylum circles and in the councils of the State and nation. Now, I say that is unfortunate, because we do not all wish to be held responsible for the opinions of that organ, or the editors of that paper. The editors of that paper have a perfect right to state what views they choose. They have a perfect right to adopt any one of them and when they choose; but it strikes me some of the methods they use are hurtful to this body.

The charge is that we are obstructionists. They may think something like this: Remarks of members of the Association meetings are published in that journal, and published for the Association. *Ergo*, it is the organ of the Association. It is false logic when it is known that the very reverse are the views of our people. It is not the fair thing to send out matter through the world as conclusive where there are different experiences on the subject close at home. It is just that sort of thing that gives a color to the charge of these people, that we are obstructionists, when the only journal at all identified with us deems it best to do this, and occasionally other things in the same way.

New reforms are of two kinds, conservative and destructive. It is well always to look about and see wherein we can set our houses in better order, and there to make conservative reforms, which act upon the principle both of acting upon new laws which are good, and of referring to the principles which have held heretofore. If we do not act thus in the nature of God's providences, we do not accept conservative reforms. Destructive reforms cut up and sweep away both the good and the bad, until after a season the dry land appears, and a harvest is reaped again. It is for this reason that I have made my remarks so extended. I do not shout "Great is Diana of the Ephesians" by any means; but I wish to say that we should each look into the whole truth, and practice it in our lives. The best sort of reform is that made from within, and if we all do that, I do not think it matters who attacks us—whether it be the highest or the lowest. I think it better we should be sure of our foundations before we attempt to rout the supposed enemy, especially as that enemy has taken the offensive. We can bear everything as long as we can say we have never blushed before.

Dr. GRAY. Mr. President and Members of the Association: In regard to the paper of Dr. Everts, which has been sufficiently discussed, the fact that I was named in the paper or referred to as a person representing the typical element of this Association, as a superintendent, might make it seem proper that I should say nothing in regard to it. It is a fact that, thus far in the history of these assailments that have been made—if they are to be called assailments—or proclamations of reform—if they are to be so designated—I have never uttered a word or made a comment. It might seem proper that I should still be silent. Dr. Macdonald has said that he knows these persons from whom the quotations are made by Dr. Everts, and who originated the attacks on asylums—or most of them—and he has given you his estimate of their character and qualifications. I have never had the personal acquaintance of Mr. Eaton, and he has never been at the asylum. Few of the persons referred to or who constitute the circle or class to which Dr. Everts and Dr. Macdonald have especially referred, have ever been inside of the institution at Utica. Mr. Eaton, their spokesman, has never addressed a line to me on any subject, and I have never had any correspondence with any of them. I therefore only know them by what I have seen in the newspapers or in the pamphlets and various circulars received from time to time, and these, I confess, have been many. I stand here to say that I have never seen a statement from these persons in any of the newspapers or in any pamphlets that I have ever received from any of them, that has ever suggested a new or valuable idea. What they have uttered of truth, touching asylum management, &c., has been the rewording of what was already well known to men of experience, or already incorporated, either in the laws, or in the rules and regulations of institutions, or in the published propositions of this Association. No advice that they have ever given me, I can safely say, is worth the paper on which it is written. What they have said in regard to me, personally, is on record as they wish it, and there may rest, as far as I am concerned. What is important and valuable for the public to know, concerning the organization and government of the State asylums, may be found incorporated in the statutes and in the by-laws which are authorized by the statutes. Apart from the personal attacks, the fault-finding and complaints have been largely directed against the lunacy laws and the regulations organizing and governing the State institutions. The general remarks of my friend Dr. Gundry, in regard to "asylum reforms," "favorable movements in our behalf," etc., and "walls of stone" as against advancement, can not apply to the State of New York, for the statutes and regulations there contain no provisions and lack no guarantees which would justify any such inference. He was evidently speaking from experience, unless he was iterating simply the sentiments of those to whom Dr. Everts has referred, and those of whom he himself speaks when he reminds the Association that "they" have the advantage of being on the offensive. Who are "they?" The "supposed enemy that has taken the offensive," and who charged "that we are obstructionists?" He knows them and he knows what they think of us. It is true in his arraignment he did not seem to like to mention the names of States or persons, but after all he mentioned himself, at least by implication, as one of the many who had suffered, and he fairly disclosed what State he had in his mind—that State being Ohio, where the Association of "Protection" to which Dr. Everts has referred was christened, if not born. Notwithstanding the concealment of names I insist, by this very fact he has intimated, that the evils he suggested or hinted at were more widely spread than the State of Ohio alone. His intimation is that we of the Association ought to answer their complaints whether the things they propose have any real substance or not, and ought to welcome them. He shakes his head at this. I claim and will here say that only such things as require answer should be so met. Mere assertions should not be met by argument. Until something is said having substance we need no argument, and we know that even one of a certain class of persons is said to be wiser than ten men who can render a reason. But mere assertions and personal attacks are not worthy of argument, and no gentleman is going to defend himself against such general detraction. The man who gives himself up to personalities and detraction and envy; who makes these the basis of any proposition of reform or conceals them behind propositions of reform, places himself beyond the pale of reputable criticism, and should be left to himself without argument or answer, where he will die under the weight of his own defamatory work, sooner or later. As far as the truth goes we accept it, but, gentlemen, I have never felt that in any of the personal assailments of myself, there was any real arraignment of this Association. I have never felt it my duty to drag anything relating to myself into this Association, or into the JOURNAL, to which Dr. Gundry has alluded. This Association is a body not especially concerned in any individual; a body that consists to be sure of individuals, but only as they represent official life and action and offices. It is always concerned primarily with the good management of all the institutions of this great country of America, that includes the Dominion of Ontario in which we now are. It does not intend, therefore, either to build up or to drag down, or to defend the mere personal interests of men. It has to do with superintendents in their public duties and capacities; it has to do with the laws which govern these institutions and the great principles which underlie them. It has done great and good work in organizing a wise and humane system, and in laying down rules and laws for the founding and government of institutions. Its first work was the bringing together men of experience and the formulation of scattered knowledge into definite propositions for discussion and guidance. These propositions containing the united experience of the men who were charged with the care of the asylums, public and private, have been added to from time to time. As Dr. Hughes has forcibly said, the great work of reform and advancement has been the work of the men of this Association. They commenced with the problem of organization under the illumination of experience, and not the mere vagaries of imagination and these men—the fathers whom Dr. Workman has so eloquently brought before us in his admirable memoir, were not visionaries or idlers; they were great practical men who organized a system, and at the outset laid down a series of propositions upon which to base their action and their efforts for genuine reform, which embraced the elevation and amelioration of the condition of the insane; and history will clearly show that nearly all the steps of real progress in this great cause were the results of consultation and discussion in their annual meetings. Since that time, from year to year, as experience has taught us their work has been enlarged, and the series of propositions and special resolutions of this body stand now to-day untouched by the sophistry of a single one of all the would-be reformers. My friend Dr. Gundry shakes his head. I repeat, not a single proposition has been gainsaid or overturned. They stand to-day above all contradiction as a part of the constitution, so to speak, of this body, and they are interwoven as a part of the fabric of our laws and their practical application is felt in all parts of the country.

Now in regard to one point. I shall dismiss all that relates to personal defense in reference to anything contained in Dr. Everts' paper, or in regard to anything that may have been said here. I do this especially because of being mentioned from beginning to end as the representative object of these attacks. I do not complain of this on the part of Dr. Everts. This personality is not his work. He has merely reproduced, in a collected way, samples of what has been uttered by others. It is only a reproduction, a condensation of the utterances of a class of men who for a time hold themselves in the public view, and I have nothing further to say about them. Their utterances are not new to me or to any of us. We have heard them *in extenso*, and the ideas repeated in all forms of expression and in all sorts of places. They have produced and reproduced each other's utterances, so as to make themselves as numerous and universal as possible. They have been given a circulation far and wide in every direction, and I am willing to take the consequences of leaving them where they are.

However, I will address myself to some points involved in the paper read by Dr. Workman, and to the remarks of Dr. Gundry, who seems, for the present, to stand as an apologist for complaints which have been made from time to time against this Association and asylums generally. Dr. Everts' paper goes to show that these "reformers" are inimical to this Association, and their statements misrepresent its expressed and recorded views.

The question in regard to the organization of asylums and the laws which govern them, as well as their character, the modes of appointment of officers and all management, inspection, visitation and internal administration, are legitimate matters of discussion, and Dr. Workman has clearly brought out the Canadian system, and I shall examine the question of the application of the Canadian and English systems, so far, at least, as the State of New York is concerned.

Now, inspection, Dr. Gundry seems to intimate, would have saved the State he referred to. He shakes his head. I agree with him; but his language, I think, would bear the signification. He has asserted "political control" and "improper trustees" as the evils which have prevailed there. What, I ask him, then, is the element of reform which would have saved the twenty-eight revolutions in a single State in a few years? He has not given us the key to this extraordinary State policy, but we should heed the lesson which it teaches us, to guard against a similar evil in any other State. If we should refuse to take such a lesson from any quarter, we should indeed be blind and unwise. Let him show us how such evils came about, and what has led that State into such a system of government so unwise and short-sighted. Let him admit the light into that darkness. This Association is not responsible for that State or its policy, or the policy or politics of any State. That is a style of government supervision with a vengeance; and the vengeance falls, as Dr. Gundry has so feelingly described, alike on the faithful and on the faithless. This is reform from without.

But we are told that all the evils that Dr. Gundry and others have referred to, are avoided in England; that all we have to do is to adopt her laws and her methods, and be at peace; that she is far ahead of us with her code of wise laws and wholesome regulations that move her charities like clockwork; that her system combines such power and means of inspection and inspectors, that the institutions move serenely along without let or hindrance or the trouble of legislation or legislative investigations, or any public challenge of their fitness or work. Is this so?

Dr. GUNDRY. Nobody said that.

Dr. GRAY. I do not say you did. Such, however, has been the

tenor of the advice from the " reformers," to whom your remarks point. Gentlemen, it would be illusive to take refuge in English methods against such men. The same class of malcontents are in England as here, and the same kind of protection societies and perturbators. Dr. Gundry has referred to Mr. Eaton's efforts, for though he says he does not intend to give names, still he certainly gives Mr. Eaton's figures of speech ; of walls of stone and hedgings in—about asylums—therefore, he has really referred, by implication, to New York, and by inference, we may assume that he believes in agitation there. Certainly, reform, however needed, has not begun in the State Dr. Gundry refers to, unless it consists in turning the wheel with the twenty-seven superintendents in the hopper, and the man who is safest comes out last. [Laughter.] He does not refer to that State by name, however.

Dr. GUNDRY. I did not refer to New York, at all.

Dr. GRAY. Then I will.

Dr. GUNDRY. I simply mentioned the JOURNAL.

Dr. GRAY. The JOURNAL will take care of itself. In the State of New York is where Dr. Everts paper locates the *nidus* or the Hades—call it what you choose—from whence radiate the "reformers." That we, in New York, have the choice central spirits, and that they are the ones we should have wooed to quiet, by argument. Alas, argument! Why not say place? It is said that they have called and we have not answered ; that we have rejected these philanthropists who were endeavoring to cast a gentle mantle of shelter over all superintendents, and who meant no evil ; wished only to inaugurate a great reform in our behalf ; that we have actually ignored them. So the Association has, and with wisdom, might do so still. As I have before said, they have not presented anything, as yet, for this Association to consider ; have not suggested anything new, or that has not been discussed in this body over and over. What *work* have they themselves done on which to claim a hearing? New York was the field for commencing operations, which were then to extend into all the States, although managers were not political speculators and superintendents in that State, had not been turned out over and over again, as in the State formerly referred to. From their representations, it would seem that the public were blind ; that they could not see the great wrongs committed ; that by some sort of magic the people had been lulled into a security which was false ; that the superintendents had thrown a glamor over everything, so that the people did not care for the evils, and therefore the officials were allowed to remain and go on unchecked in their iniquitous wrongs; that they were so secure that no charges could affect them; that the institutions were so inclosed and secluded that no persons could even peep into the windows; that they were so privately fortified that they could not be overcome; that there was a ring encircling and holding this accumulated power and influence. Into this ring only the chosen were admitted, while the empty-stomached outsiders, anxious and weary in waiting and hoping, were all uncomfortable and unhappy because kept away. [Laughter.] In this ring were included all asylum authorities, all the numerous managers who were in and all who went in from time to time—they were all changed at once into adherents and ring men the moment they were brought within this strange and mysterious influence. (I see one of them, Mr. Ogden, of the Willard Asylum, here.) This magic power extended to any who received appointments, no matter what their former position or influence or character or place in State affairs or society. To be sure the managers were amongst the most reputable men of the State, occupying the high places, judges, lawyers, physicians, bankers, presidents of railroads, men of business and of all affairs; but they at once, when brought within this magic influence of this ring, were transformed. Furthermore, the moment the Legislature took hold of the matter of insanity and asylums, and the members tried to comprehend this same question, they also became infatuated in the same way. Who was the magician? What was the magic wand that did all this? The magician was the law and the wand was truth and justice. It was the completeness of the law, and the untruthfulness of the defamatory assertions. [Applause.] Truth, with its illumination standing in contrast with misrepresentation, ignorance, malice. The law, with its embodiment of wise, just and humane provisions against the foolish utterances of theorists and malcontents; New York law: "feeble and incongruous!" Can you set argument against words? It would only be beating the air. It was no man and no set of men that thwarted these evil efforts. When pointed out they tell of their own weakness. When legislators came to look at what the law really was, and what the practice really was, under the law, and came to inquire into the declarations of the assailants, they saw that their assertions were without foundation. That is all there was of it.

We now come to the question of inspection. Dr. Workman has very clearly set forth what the inspection and government of the Canadian institutions consists in. Dr. Gundry declares that this would satisfy him. He also admits and even declares that the powers and duties of the General Inspector of Canada, Mr. Langmuir, is simply the power and duties conferred upon boards of managers in certain of the States. No one has objected to inspection, and there is really no essential difference between the Canadian system and that of New York. (I do not represent other States here.) In Canada the inspector is the appointed agent and representative of the government in managing, visiting and more or less moulding the government of the institutions. Acting thus in an advisory way with the superintendents in a common effort, and stimulating them by coöperative government aid in all their work.

The boards of managers in the State of New York represent the same power. The government of the State asylums is by special statute "vested in the board of managers;" that is, each institution has a board charged with the complete government, inspection and visitation. Surely we have in New York, therefore, a body of inspectors in the very sense in which Dr. Workman has represented them in his paper, equal to all our needs. We have sixty men as managers and inspectors of the State asylums, and I will say here in regard to this that you can not take one out of them and put the stain upon him that Dr. Gundry has put upon the managers in the State he alludes to. I have been connected for thirty years with one institution, and I have never heard a word in regard to contracts or politics in the board there whatever the changes have been, nor have I ever heard a trustee or manager suggesting political favoritism, or any favoritism, or the appointment of any one except under the strictest provisions of law.

Dr. GUNDRY. Will the Doctor allow me a single remark? You said the State alluded to was Ohio.

Dr. GRAY. I did not say Ohio. What I did say was that you referred to the State of Ohio.

Dr. GUNDRY. Before the reporters of the press leave I hope the reference to that State will be stricken out, because I drew my inferences from various States. I did not want to and I do not want the Doctor to allow it to refer to any State—so if the reporters will strike that out they will oblige me. If I did seemingly refer to Ohio I did not intend it.

Dr. GRAY. He has referred to something within his personal knowledge or beyond it. If it is within the State of Ohio he has personal knowledge. But whether or not he alluded to that State, such flagrant charges should be located and not asserted to the disparagement of institutions, and of managers of institutions in all the States. Managers are not here to defend themselves, and besides, I desire to locate his inferences as far as possible. This Association is not for the trial of managers or for the discussion of politics. The managers or management of these great institutions should not be attacked on mere inferences. In every State there is a tribunal for these things and they ought to be there relegated. Innuendo is not letting in the light. But I will apply more fully now what I have said upon this point. I never have had a suggestion for an appointment, from the lowest position to the highest, from the board of managers or any members of it. I have never heard of a ripple towards influencing appointments. The laws are so complete, so plain, and the duties so well defined in regard to everything, every duty, that no man need make a mistake unless he does it without regard to the spirit, or letter of these laws; and the rules and regulations are definite and clear in regard to the respective duties of all officers and all persons employed. So much have I said in regard to managers for the reason that Dr. Gundry has here assailed them, and in this respect has put himself into the shoes of the reformers run mad. I will say more. I take it the rule is about the same over the United States as to boards of managers. Take the State of New York—and I am not afraid to mention my State—these boards are composed of lawyers, doctors, and business men of capacity, in every institution, who are appointed by the Governor and confirmed by the Senate of the State as being suitable persons to assume the trust—for it is a position of trust—the carrying out of the statutes looking after the interests of the State and the welfare of her insane citizens. The service is rendered gratuitously. They report annually to the Legislature and the reports are open to the inspection of legislators, of the Governor, and anybody else who wishes to look at them. These managers are amenable to the Governor as his appointees. He can arrest them in any evil course at any time, bring them before him and suspend them, and the Senate can remove them if they do wrong. Has the law here given no safeguards?

Now as to direct governmental power the Governor can go in person, or send any one to represent him, to any State institution to inspect and inquire. That has been done in the State of New York on the representation of one Chambers, a newspaper correspondent, as we know very well in regard to Bloomingdale, a few years ago; and the Governor did not then confine inquiries to

Bloomingdale. He ordered the commission to go to every institution in the State, whether there were complaints or not, to see whether any person was improperly confined or detained, or whether there were any wrongs existing to be redressed; that board consisted of Dr. Thomas Hun, of Albany, the Attorney General of the State, General Barlow, and President Anderson, of the Rochester University, who was then President of the State Board of Charities. The profession was ably represented by Dr. Hun, the State in the Attorney General, and the State Board of Charities in its president. That commission went all over the State into every institution, public and private. They were untrammeled and impartial men, but they received no credit from the class of unhappy "reformers" because they found no evils.

Dr. GUNDRY. But from the people they did.

Dr. GRAY. The people had never murmured. Those gentlemen reported to the Legislature, but the cry soon went up from the same class of complainers that somebody had befogged them. Now were those men dependent upon the superintendents of the various institutions or the managers? Had they any of the embarrassments referred to concerning inspection or visitation? No. They went through the institutions with independence and a fearless disregard of everything, except the duties they were to perform under their appointment. But we not only have the Governor with power, but the Comptroller of the State can inquire at any time into the finances of any State institution; can himself visit them and examine, or send any person whom he chooses, just as the inspector of this province can enter any institution. But we have also a special Commissioner in Lunacy, an able lawyer and jurisprudent. He has not been in power for a day, but for seven years. He has visited all the institutions freely and untrammeled, and has made his reports annually to the Legislature. In addition we have the State Board of Charities, which has had among its members such able organizers as Hon. Theodore W. Dwight, of the Law School, Dr. M. B. Anderson, President of Rochester University and Hon. J. V. L. Pruyn. Have they found the statutes "weak and incongruous?"

Now it is not to the discredit of the institutions of the State of New York, or to the provisions of these statutes, that these officers have not turned things upside down every time a clamor is made, or some one wants a place as in the case stated by Dr. Gundry. But apart from all this the institutions are all under the immediate control of the Legislature; they are in every sense creatures of the law and the managers are legislative agents to see that the great trust committed to them is properly discharged.

One unfamiliar with the law except as expounded by Mr. Eaton might imagine that no attention had ever been paid to this subject in the State of New York. A few years ago it was thought that as our laws in regard to the insane were scattered over so vast a field—of seventy years or more—that many of those coming into office from time to time throughout the State could not know what the laws were, and the Legislature immediately directed them codified and put into form as a lunacy code, and this was ordered to be done by the Attorney General of the State, then an eminent lawyer and judge or one who had been a judge, and the State Commissioner in Lunacy. This was only as far back as 1874. For those who really wish to be informed there are no obstacles in the way of information. There is no reason for the ignorant and misleading statements as to the statutes of New York which have been made such a bugbear and outcry. There has been no difficulty, on the other hand, either in ascertaining what the system of England is or has been. In her provisions for lunacy, apart from her statutes, by reading the reports and especially those of the Commissioners in Lunacy themselves, the system and practice are readily ascertained. I have long taken an interest in the subject, having read most of the English lunacy reports, and if the Inspector, the Hon. Mr. Langmuir, will allow me to say so, when he was first appointed Inspector for Canada and visited our State in his primary inquiries into the subject, he gave me quite an impetus to the study of the provisions of the English statutes, and I naturally felt interested to know how, in working out the great problem of caring for the insane, we could utilize the experience embodied in the system of England. I found in Great Britain they have not the same laws everywhere. The English law differs from that of Ireland or Scotland; yet they are all on the order of local self-government. They believe as we believe here that people can be found in every part of every great State quite competent to manage their local affairs, and to guard the interests and rights of their citizens whether sane or insane. Dr. Gundry talks about a national board. Why, a national board could not enter States in the management of beneficiary and charitable affairs. The charities of States are their own affairs.

Now, so far as the State of New York has been named, I have a right to speak, and especially as Mr. Eaton has set up New York as the typical State, the laws of which he seems to hold, are enacted for the oppression of the insane, and not for their good. If his accusations against the State of New York are not true, his whole fabric falls to the ground, for he has made that the representative State. I say this, although my friend, Dr. Gundry, shakes his head, and he probably has read the article of Mr. Eaton much more carefully than I have. But the article shows, and certainly Dr. Everts has shown, that Utica was used as the illustration. When Mr. Eaton appeared before the Legislature, heralded by the free distribution of pamphlets and strips of printed matter, setting forth what it was claimed the laws of the State were, and the changes needed, without giving the actual statutes or even quoting from the mass of statutes, he especially endeavored to show that what was lacking was a large body of commissioners like the Lunacy Commission of England, with their powers and their duties and the class of men who there occupied those positions; that short of such a commission and such power and such men, we were a failure, and should not and could not succeed. I also listened to his verbal argument and to the remarks of those with him, and had all taken down. Among the main points put forth was, that in England this large board had great wisdom, and especially power to guard against abuses and to right wrongs; that in the great private and public institutions there, the power lodged in this board had not only an influence that was wonderful by their very majesty, but they had the power of giving speedy redress; on the other hand, that in New York, all this was wanting; the logical inference being that we were weak in all that in which they were strong; that the English board had lawyers for legal affairs, physicians for medical matters and business men for ordinary affairs; the logical inference being that our Managers, Commissioner in Lunacy, &c., were not such men. He failed to say that under the Statutes of New York, no delay is ever necessary; that our laws are such that our courts can be applied to and are always sitting at our very doors; he might have said that in justice and in truth, but he did not. He might also, had he simply opened his eyes to the facts before him, have said that in the several boards of managers of the asylums in New York, we have precisely the same class of men, lawyers, physicians and business men, as there are in the English Com-

missiou, but he did not.* Without going specifically into the
matter, I might add that when one came to look at his declarations, it was apparent that his representation of the powers and
duties of the English Commission was misleading, and it was easy
for the Legislature to see by consulting the English Statutes, that
they had no such power as he pretended. Lord Shaftesbury, who
had been for fifty years at the head of that commission, said, before
the Committee of Parliamentary, in 1877, (and could Mr. Eaton
have been ignorant of this?) "we, in visiting asylums, have no
power at all, except to examine and report." He declared, em-
phatically, "we have never exercised any authority; we have
never had any to exercise, and it would be most unadvisable to
give us any authority." His Lordship further declared that in
regard to supervision, inspection and visitation of asylums, he
would rather increase local authorities, because they had great advantages in knowing the character of the patients, the character
of the superintendent, and can judge far better, and added:
"Above all things, they have the power in their hands." Was
Lord Shaftesbury right, or Mr. Eaton wrong?

The only "incongruous" thing shown by Mr. Eaton was in the act
converting the Inebriate Asylum at Binghamton into an asylum
for the chronic insane, which, he said, "Gives no sphere of duty
whatever to the Commissioner in Lunacy." It is proper to say
that this enactment was subsequent to the lunacy code, and while
an attack was being made on the State Commissioner in Lunacy—
an attempt to obliterate the office.

---

* " We see, therefore, with what sedulous care this law has provided for
the three distinct varieties of experience and ability upon this National
Board of Commissioners. Five men of affairs to supply business capacity—
three barristers, learned in the law and experienced in the courts of justice,
to keep the Board within legal limits—three physicians and surgeons, to
supply medical and surgical science and skill. The prestige and capacity
which such a body brings to the investigation of lunatic asylums, and the
weight which its recomendations naturally carry, must be obvious without
more words upon the subject."

" The statutory directions for visitations, inspections and investigations on
the part of the Commissioners are in the highest degree stringent and particular, and the power given to make them efficient is most ample. * * *
Their power further extends to visitations, inspections and taking effective
measures for relief in cases where the insane suffers wrong in jails, work-
houses and other places in the kingdom."

" No one can read it without a painful sense of the defective, feeble and
incongruous laws of New York upon the same subject."

DORMAN B. EATON.

Touching England's state institutions, in regard to visitations, rules, regulations, &c., the Commissioners have nothing to do with them. Their state institutions, those for the army, for the navy, &c., are visited once a year by the Commissioners, by courtesy, while all the rules and regulations for their government are under the departments which they represent; not made by the Commissioners at all, but by the managing boards, precisely as under the Statutes of New York. But there are certain other institutions called, in English law, asylums, which are the borough and county institutions, similar to our State institutions. Are they organized or managed or controlled by the Commissioners of Lunacy there? Not at all. Those institutions have their own laws and they have their local boards and local visitors, and then they have inspection once a year by the Commissioners, but without power, as the Commissioners say, except to visit and report. They are visited precisely as the institutions of New York are visited by the Commissioner in Lunacy and by the State Board of Charities, and the institutions are governed and controlled by their local or managing boards, just as the State asylums are in New York by the boards of managers. Now, you come to still another class of English institutions, called hospitals for the insane, and I desire to say that I am adhering rigidly to what the law there says, and not to newspapers, these institutions, which are similar to Bloomingdale, New York, and the Pennsylvania Hospital for the Insane, are described as hospital buildings, or part of a hospital or house not being an asylum, where lunatics are received by benevolent contributions in part or in whole, or by charitable bequests, and where some persons pay more than their support, the balance going to the charitable care of all. Here the Commissioners in Lunacy have no control. They visit them just as the Commissioner in Lunacy does in New York, but with a good deal less power than he has. What public institutions have they in England further where insane are kept? They have work-houses, and within the walls of the work-houses of England there are now over 16,000 insane. The Commissioners in Lunacy simply visit them all, but they have no control over them. They are absolutely under the local authorities.* The English statutes do not even require certificates of insanity for the commitment of the insane to these work-houses.

---

*Lord Shaftesbury says: "In respect to the county asylums and to work-houses we are merely a body to inspect and to report. We have no authority at all except in the special case of finding lunatics therein who ought to be sent to asylums."

Where is all the talk, therefore, about the weakness of New York law, and about the superiority of England over the State of New York? England herself has made no pretentions to this. Now, the work-houses are represented as asylums the same as our city asylums and county asylums may be so represented. They are all independent institutions and governed as local institutions, and they are scattered all through England precisely as the chronic insane poor are in the poor-houses of our States and in our municipal institutions. Now, are we better off or worse off in respect to the supervision or visitation of this class of institutions than England is? We really exercise more State power directly over them than England has yet done over her similar institutions. Why, the local authorities in the State of New York, the counties, can not take care of the chronic insane among the helpless, ordinary poor as they do in England, without having a license to do so from the State Board of Charities, or a direct legislative permissive act in each case, and our Commissioner in Lunacy must accept the character of the buildings in which they are proposed to be kept by the counties.

Now, in regard to private asylums, Mr. Eaton, before the legislative committee, said: with a great Board of Commissioners, they could regulate the capacity of such institutions and all that sort of thing in England and Wales, while in New York there was no one to look after them. In England and Wales there are about one hundred private institutions. In New York there are not over five, all told, and they contain—leaving out Bloomingdale, an old chartered institution—a mere handful of patients, and these institutions are licensed by the State Commissioner in Lunacy, and visited and inspected by him. Did Mr. Eaton know this? The English Commissioners in Lunacy are charged with the duty of licensing and inspecting certain private asylums, and in some sense representing the interests of the insane poor who are kept within the control of such institutions. For they are allowed to receive pauper insane, and the Statutes of England declare them to be private asylums where private or pauper insane are taken for care and treatment as a speculation by the proprietors. It is but reasonable that the State should step in as a police to guard and protect the civil rights of the patients there, so that when the government has granted this privilege to the citizen of speculative care of its helpless ones their civil rights may, nevertheless, be constantly guarded by the State as represented by these Commissioners. They do not and can not license any institution beyond thirteen months, and in order to keep that continued watchfulness over them they are visited six times a year, or as often as is necessary, to see that they serve the very purposes for which they were created; but their State institutions and the corporate and borough asylums which are allied to our State and municipal institutions are not regulated by the Commissioners, for all their duties are simply visitorial and advisory, and they are all regulated and governed by the local Commissioners which represent our boards of managers and trustees, and there these boards, justices and visitors of the various places make the appointments precisely as they are made in New York by managers and commissioners. Even the authority of licensing by the English Commissioners in Lunacy is limited to a metropolitan area within seven miles around London, Westminster and Southwark, which does not embrace half the private institutions. Throughout all the rest of England and Wales they are licensed by the justices of the counties or boroughs at quarter or general sessions. Talk about national boards and national interference with States! In England they are such sticklers for local authority that no justice is permitted to visit any institution except that which he has himself licensed. There the Commissioners can not even revoke a license. This can only be done by the Lord Chancellor. Within the metropolitan district the licensed houses receive six visits of the Commissioners. Outside of this district they receive the same number from the local visitors appointed by the justices and two visits a year by the Commissioners, whereas the lunatic hospitals receive but one visit a year from the Commissioners.

Thus it will be seen what respect the English government pays to the principle of local government, in all matters where there is taxation for the support of individuals in her institutions; and also to another great principle of having the real powers that govern and direct her charitable affairs so near the institutions to be governed that they will not only know all about them, but where they can be instantly called in case of emergency.

Why should the New York statutes so resemble the English statutes? The organic law of lunacy of the State of New York to organize its system of State institutions was drawn by some of the ablest lawyers of the State—at the head of these John C. Spencer, assisted by that able jurisprudent, Dr. Beck, who was for many years one of the managers of the Utica Asylum. These men did not fail to consult any wholesome provision already in existence in England or elsewhere, and gave them therefore all the safeguards that they could. No great changes have been made in the English statutes or in the organization and management of English institutions since that time setting out guarantees for the safety and liberty of the subject or the humane care of the insane that we have not recognized; certainly there are none existent now that outstrip the safeguards provided by the statutes of the State of New York.

In the report of the Parliamentary Committee of 1877, to which allusion has been made, it is declared that New York, in the legislation of 1874, has carefully guarded against improper commitments, and that in no other State besides New York, is the approval of a court, in regard to medical certificates, necessary, thus guaranteeing entire safety and certainty as to medical certificates and their *judicial approval* in the commitment of the insane to her institutions.

Dr. GUNDRY. They made a mistake. There are other States.

Dr. GRAY. I am stating now what the Parliamentary Committee said, as well as talking to the proposition which Dr. Gundry himself urged we were not meeting—the proposition for advancement, for he claimed really that we were going backwards. I desire to show that whatever State is going backwards, New York is not. It may be asked whether the laws of New York really afford the guarantees we claim as to the rights of her citizens. In addition to the fact that the law requires that the certificate shall be made by medical men having certain qualifications, which qualifications are to be approved by a court of record before they can examine an insane person for commitment, the judge or court before approving any certificate, may in his discretion, call a jury to decide as to the insanity. Are rights not guaranteed? But we really may ask is the removal of an insane person to a hospital the taking away of rights? They are sent to institutions simply because they are sick. There is no right taken away permanently. A distinguished justice once said in a case where the question came up as to the right of commitment to an asylum of a wife by her husband: "It is not a right taken away from this woman, but is a right given to her, a right that she shall be treated properly and be defended against her disease and herself." Nevertheless it is eminently proper that the best possible guarantees shall be given by the profession as is done in the State of New York. What are the guarantees that the law demands before a man shall present himself as a medical examiner to commit an insane person in the State of New York? Every physician before he can act as an examiner in lunacy for the commitment of an insane person to any place is required to be a graduate of some regularly incorporated institution, a citizen of the State, a permanent resident of the State; he shall have practiced at least three years in his profession; he shall be a man of reputable character, and all this shall be shown to the satisfaction of a court of record before such court can certify him as a legal examiner. With the certification of such a record he has the right and authority to examine. Now he must also personally examine the patient, and within a reasonable time before commitment, the law fixing this time within ten days of sending the person to the asylum. But the law goes still further. Unwilling to leave even the form of such certificate to the caprice of the physician it declares that the certificates they sign shall be made in accordance with a form prescribed by the Commissioner in Lunacy, and the medical examiner is not only required to give an opinion setting forth the insanity, but also to state the grounds upon which that opinion rests, in the body of the certificate, and this certificate is required to be under oath, and there must be two of them in every case, and these certificates, as before stated, must have the approval, in writing, of the judge of the county where the patient resides or of a justice of the Supreme Court. Is there any other State that gives such guarantees as to the rights of citizens ? Among the important questions which were brought before the Parliamentary Committee already referred to, was that of medical certificates. In England but one certificate is required, and the qualification demanded of the physicians are by no means up to the requirements of the statute of New York, and instead of the judicial approval of the New York certificates the English certificates simply require to be ratified or approved by the Commissioners. On the question of judicial approval Lord Shaftesbury was rather opposed to it, and on the ground that such approval would carry with it the protection of the physician; that he would be protected from prosecution for this professional act by the judge's approval, all of which would be so and very properly. If a medical man is called upon to discharge such an act towards his fellow-man he should be protected, and in fact the large responsibility of commitment of the insane under certificates rests directly with the medical profession, which certainly would not be less careful, anticipating such judicial action.

Now 1 submit that these points embodied in the statutes of New York represent everything in the British statutes that are of value in the government of institutions and the commitment and detention of persons therein ; that all that is beneficial and useful is represented in the statutes of New York as fully as those in any realm or government in this world. I do not deem it neccessary to defend the statutes. They are records to be read by all men if they choose to read. I have said thus much mainly out of compliment to the able paper of my friend, Dr. Workman, and to meet the questions of Dr. Gundry and only incidentally to show that the foundation upon which the assertions of Mr. Eaton and others were made was not sound. Mr. Eaton really answered himself as Dr. Everts has shown.

It is safe to say that had Mr. Eaton and those for whom he was spokesman, and those who appeared with him, been as industrious and persevering in the study of the law, and in informing themselves of the various provisions that really existed touching the institutions, as well as their workings and management, as they were in the opposite direction, in building up their baseless theories and in personal attacks, they might have accomplished some good to themselves if not to others. It was only after Mr. Eaton had failed to impress the Legislature with his representations and interpretations of the statutory provisions of New York, that he resorted to the *North American Review* to pour out his wrath and grievances to a wider audience. However, as Dr. Everts has sufficiently shown, with regard to the pamphleteers generally, the coarse manner of the attack, the crudity of their ideas, and the gross personalities together presented evidence of an animus well calculated to antidote any evil in the minds of unprejudiced and intelligent readers. Still it may be true that the iteration and re-iteration, uncontradicted, of the most baseless scandal may injure institutions, as we know it does the reputations of individuals. Dr. Macdonald has given an illustration of Mr. Eaton's style of inquiry and fairness.

Gentlemen, I have detained you too long. I did not intend to say a word upon this subject and should not have said anything but that the matter was taken up really by our friend Dr. Gundry. Now a word in regard to the JOURNAL OF INSANITY, which seems to disturb him. When it can not take care of itself it will have to go to the wall. [Laughter and applause]. For their own opinions its editors are responsible and not the Association. Members of the Association are responsible for their own utterances. Dr. Gundry has said that it was not the organ of this body. No one has claimed this. It has published for a number of years the official proceedings of the Association under a resolution of this body, and it has faithfully carried out the provisions of that reso-

lution. It has never made a comment upon any part of the proceedings of the Association or upon the remarks of any member
therein contained. The editor of the JOURNAL is a member of this
Association, and has never felt himself hampered in any way by
any relations he has held to the JOURNAL, and in no instance has
he ever dragged it before the Association for favor or disfavor,
and he will not be led now into any controversy or any reply to
the attempted strictures of Dr. Gundry.

Dr. WORKMAN. I have no desire—having read my paper yesterday—to introduce an apple of discord; but I do not regret now
that I did read that paper. It has given me the pleasure of hearing some very eloquent speeches.

I think Dr. Gray's observations tend to confirm what I advanced yesterday in regard to our governmental system of inspection. The difference between Dr. Gray's plan and mine is simply
this: Mine would be only the one man power, or it might be two
or three for a whole State, while the New York system has a
large board of inspection and management for their institutions.
The Doctor has certainly proved that the institutions of New
York have been well taken care of; and one proof of this is that
he has been for thirty years in one institution. Had a different
plan existed, and the work of the inspector became a tenure, I
think we should have seen a dozen Dr. Grays in Utica since he has
been there. I think the more administrative and inspection power
the better. I know that our friend Mr. Langmuir, who has for
some fourteen years filled the office of inspector, and has now a
number of institutions under his care, finds them more efficiently
worked than ever and his time most thoroughly taken up. I
think, however, it would be much better for him to have an asso-
ciate. The difference between the criminal insane and insane not
criminals, is such that to have the supervision of both devolve
upon Mr. Langmuir so different in their character, is not as desirable as it would be to have them separated. I do not think the
other institutions of this country should be under the same management as a criminal institution. When the act was being framed
for an inspector I wrote to a member of the Assembly relative to
the expediency of this. He wrote to me the way matters stood
and that he would have voted for it after advocating it the way it
then was, but as I was a candidate for the office he certainly would
support my suggestion. I did not know that I was a candidate
until then.

With regard to the sixty gentlemen who visit and govern the

State institutions in the State of New York, I would ask Dr. Gray if they act as a Board of Inspection.

Dr. GRAY. Each institution has its own board, and the boards vary in number from nine to thirteen. Each institution has on its board the elements necessary for government and inspection—men of financial management, lawyers and physicians.

Dr. WORKMAN. But as I have just said, the best evidence of the efficiency of your system is the permanence of the officials of your State—to which I alluded yesterday, and the same may be said of some of the States of New England. But how is it in the west and southwest? If I should go there next year I should miss half of them; and if after ten years, I do not know that there would be a grease spot left.

Dr. GRAY. In what I have said I only claim that we are fully abreast with the best of them; but I do not by this intend to claim that we are not going to do still better. We know there are always possible elements inherent out of which we may make advancement in perfecting all laws and organization. In these problems of State policy, as in all great social questions, institutions and their organization are matters of growth, and we are not standing still, but we have grown steadily and intend to grow more in every way toward perfection.

Dr. GUNDRY. As I supposed, Dr. Gray does not propose to admit all the powers of English boards, particularly the power to require a transcript of the history of every commitment into every institution. It is required that notice of every admission shall be sent to them within ten days.

Dr. GRAY. In New York we have on this very point all the safeguards of English law, and more too. This question of certificates for commitment and power of approval was a point especially considered in the legislative codification of our Lunacy Laws in 1874. As I have already shown, the power of review and approval of the certificates is given to the county judges and justices of the Supreme Court. The certificates must be in a form prescribed by the State Commissioner in Lunacy, and must be approved in writing by a justice of the Supreme Court, or by the county judge of the county in which the lunatic resides, and must accompany the patient and be filed in the hospital as a permanent record with the history of the case. The New York statute goes farther than the English in regard to certificates of commitment and power of review and approval. First, in requiring that the medical examiners shall have certain qualifications—shall be graduates of incorporated medical colleges, practitioners of not less than three years, permanent residents of the State, and men of reputable character. Medical examiners must have an attest of these qualifications by a court of record before they are entitled to examine and make a certificate. Each examiner must make the certificate under oath, which must recite his qualifications and state the date of examination, and give the ground of his opinion, and must give also the name of the judge or justice under whose attestation he acts as an examiner. Again the justice or judge who finally reviews and approves the certificate before commitment, may, if he sees fit, summon a jury to decide as to the question of lunacy, but under no circumstances can a commitment be made unless with the judicial approval of the certificate in its form and substance. These I submit, are greater safeguards where the court appears with power of full inquiry into the case, and where he can call the physician before him or the patient either before commitment, than the sending of a transcript to commissioners who know nothing of the case further than the paper discloses, and this after the lunatic is actually admitted. As to the history of the case, the New York statute specifically directs that it shall be entered in a book kept for the purpose and written up from time to time. I do not know of a single provision of the British Lunacy Laws of any practical bearing that we have not incorporated, and some of them we have greatly improved upon, and this is an instance.